Medium Rare

to

Well Done

A true-life account of a hugely popular Medium.
Born on the wrong side of the tracks, until the spirit
world led him (eventually) to the right path.

RONNIE BUCKINGHAM

WITH

STEPHANIE MACKENTYRE

Copyright © 2024 Ronnie Buckingham All rights reserved. No portion of this book may be reproduced mechanically, electronically, or by any other means, including photocopying, without written permission of the author/publisher. It is illegal to copy this book, post it to a website, either in part or wholly, or distribute it by any other means without prior permission from the author/publisher in writing.

The moral right of the author has been asserted.

ISBN: 9798327206953

Ronnie Buckingham

Braintree, Essex United Kingdom

Book cover design by Alishba Shah

Published by Ronnie Buckingham Publishing

Limits of Liability and Disclaimer of Warranty

The author and publisher shall not be liable for your misuse of this material. This book is strictly for informational and entertainment purposes. The author and/or publisher shall have neither liability nor responsibility to anyone with respect to any loss or damage caused, or alleged to be caused, directly or indirectly by the information contained in this book.

DEDICATION

I'd like to dedicate this book to Monique, 'the beautiful and bravest of the brave' my niece who fought cancer so bravely for five years until the very end.

Also, to my father-in-law Les Jones who brightened up the lives of all who knew him, and my eldest brother Michael who I always looked up to and admired.

ACKNOWLEDGEMENTS

I couldn't have produced this book without the guidance and support of so many people including;

Andrzej Karczewski for his invaluable help with photography.

James Wilkinson for the wonderful painting he did of me, which I've got hanging at home and have also used for the cover of this latest book.

All of the many people who have bravely recounted their readings they've had with me. For sending them over as testimonials, with their blessing, for publication.

Finally, to my wife Nicky for her patience and hospitality while I held meetings at our home with my publisher and for making us endless cups of tea!

CONTENTS

FOREWARD v
INTRODUCTION ix
CHAPTER 1 1
HEALING HANDS 1
CHAPTER 2 11
A MOTHER'S LOVE 11
CHAPTER 3 37
FATHERS 37
CHAPTER 4 51
PETS 51
CHAPTER 5 69
LOSING MY OWN LOVED ONES 69
CHAPTER 6 109
SIBLING BONDS 109
CHAPTER 7 113
SPIRIT CHILDREN 113
CHAPTER 8 127
FIGHTING FIT 127
CHAPTER 9 153
HUSBANDS 153
CHAPTER 10 165
A PICTURE PAINTS A THOUSAND WORDS 165
CHAPTER 11 179
A GRANDPARENT'S WISDOM 179
CHAPTER 12 207
INSIDE THE CAGE 207
CHAPTER 13 219

NO TIME TO SAY GOODBYE	219
CHAPTER 14	245
CAN A MEDIUM EVER RETIRE?	245
CHAPTER 15	255
AUNTS AND UNCLES	255
AFTERWORD	265
ABOUT THE AUTHORS	293

RONNIE BUCKINGHAM

FOREWARD

My Dad passed away in 1974, when I was 14 years old. Apart from the time I spent with my Dad, I didn't have a happy childhood and have had a lot of counselling.

Anna's Father

At the beginning of my reading with Ronnie he connected with my Dad. He told me a lot of things that neither Ronnie or my dad could have known as they'd happened after his passing.

Ronnie asked me who Leonard is - a family member. I had no idea, but a couple of weeks later, whilst looking through some papers that my cousin had sent me (my cousin has also passed, but he was a historian) these included a family tree where he had traced my Dad's family back through Belgium. It turned out my grandmother was from there. When I looked at the family tree, I could see that her maiden name was Leonarts.

I remember Ronnie made a kneading motion on the table with his hands and he said he had no idea what he was doing, but that my dad was showing you this. My dad was a Baker.

Ronnie told me that I had lots of pictures in my front room, unlike most people who have two or three, which was true. He went on to tell me that I have a picture of my dad on the wall in the front room, with him in his army uniform - which was also true. Ronnie said that although I wasn't the youngest, my dad referred to me as 'his baby', which was true. I spent a lot of time with my dad - we were inseparable.

Towards the end of the reading, Ronnie mentioned that I have two brothers, but that he didn't have a good feeling about it. He asked me why he wanted to call me Sheila - this is my mother's name. Ronnie also said that we didn't have a good relationship, and hadn't spoken for a long time, this was true.

Ronnie said that my dad had something to say, but had left it until the end to ensure that Ronnie understood him and what he was trying to say. He told me that my Dad knew that something bad had happened to me during my childhood. My Dad didn't know about it while he was alive. Ronnie said that he found it hard because he himself has three daughters. Ronnie went back to talking about my brothers again. He said that they had done something bad to me. He said that it was unusual for a spirit to give you so much detailed information. My hand was in his from across the table and then he said, "Oh my God, they raped you!" I confirmed that it was true. We were both in tears then. I think some of mine were through sheer relief that my dad knew and had believed me.

Ronnie went on to say how angry my dad was about this, and how angry he was with my mother and my sister (both had supported my brother during the historic child abuse case when it went to Court and have not spoken to me since). My Dad knew so much about the case and the relationship with my mother and sister, which is still non-existent. Ronnie told me that it was very rare for a medium to receive such detailed information and on such an awful subject. I know that it was an upsetting reading for him. For me however, it was a kind of relief for me to hear.

It gave me so much comfort, knowing that my dad was there and supporting me. I could never repay the peace that Ronnie brought to me with this reading, and also on other occasions during group readings, where my dad and other members of my family have come through.

My very best wishes

Anna

RONNIE BUCKINGHAM

INTRODUCTION

Those of you that have read *Medium Rare* my first book, will know that I have had a very dubious past. I was brought up with time in borstal, prison and that first book is all about the upbringing that I had. However, when Medium Rare first came out it was Christmas 2016, there is this image of Mediums being rather godly and in tune with spirits and generally very nice people. Of course, my worry was wow now the world knows that I've been an armed robber, I've been in prison, I've been in borstal, I've been divorced, I've womanised – basically I've done all these bad things. I've had a lifetime of being a bouncer for nightclubs, I thought how is this going to go down with my future audiences?

I had a show that month, just after the book came out. It was in a hall in Saffron Walden. I arrived and looked out at the audience and I'm pleased to say it was packed. In my life I've always believed that the best form of defense is attack. So, I marched straight down to the front of the crowd and I said, "Right who's read me fucking book?!" Nearly every hand went up. This old woman said, "What a naughty man you were Ronnie, but we bloody love ya!" At that, everyone cheered so I went on with the evening.

At the front there was an older woman sat, very smart with a very dapper man. He was short and dark in a lovely suit. I could see these energies around this woman. I said to her, "I'm coming to you, you've lost two husbands." She replied in a well-spoken voice, "I've actually lost three." I replied, "Fuck being married to you!" I said to the man next to her, he was an American, "You're going to be husband number four." He told me, "Yes I am." I continued, "Let me shake your hand Sir, with her track record, you're not going to be here for long!"

The place literally fell about laughing and that set the scene that night. I hope, as you start this second book of mine, it helps you to see who I am and how I work always with a twinkle in my eye. Always giving messages with a good dose of good humour but also with sensitivity where needed too of course. Since that night I've continued to be welcomed everywhere I go.

Here's Judi Brewis to tell you her side of the story from that night …

I have been to probably 12 of Ronnie's shows and only once did I never have someone come through. My most stand out ones are from Jaywick. Ronnie you asked the audience who had lost two husbands, so I raised my hand. You then said can you understand the name Joe? That's my now third husband John. You asked if he was on this side of life and so I said yes, but that he had recently had a stroke. To which you replied, "What's your name Jonah?!"

You went on to ask if all three were friends. I confirmed that they had been. You said, "They approved of him." You then asked if I could take that I had been a nurse or a carer, as the one talking to you said I had the biggest heart of anyone he had known. I did in fact manage a care home for ladies with Alzheimer's and Dementia. You told me that my husband wanted to say he was sorry for the way he had treated me. You said he was sorry that he stitched me up. He had secret bank accounts and money overseas that his ex-wife, an accountant, knew about and I never did. So, when he died, I never got anything.

Moving forward to four years later in Colchester, you asked again who had lost two husbands, I raised my hand. Once again asked who is Joe? I told you it's John my 3rd husband. You asked if I could understand that he was sick in the stomach area. He had been diagnosed the week before with stomach cancer, you then rubbed your chest and said does he have asthma or something wrong with his lungs? John also had a pulmonary embolism. You said he would be ok, it will take a while but he will be better. I am pleased to confirm that seven months later he had his op, he's done chemo and is back at work.

Another night at Jaywick watching Ronnie work, a lady came through with a message for me and said she regretted giving up her baby. My mum's sister had given her baby away to a couple who ran a cafe. She said to tell her she was proud of her but she needed to cut down on her drinking. My cousin had found her family in the mid 80's. She is an artist, but she is also an alcoholic.

God bless

Judi x

CHAPTER 1

HEALING HANDS

I have recently had an operation on my knee and as I write this I'm hobbling about on crutches. It's not stopped me doing my shows though or made me lose my sense of humour. I tottered into a show only last week on my crutches and as they all looked up at me I said, "Anyone seen a parrot?!" They all just burst out laughing.

When I first began as a medium, I found I could also heal people as well. It's not something I do these days as I was told it was literally draining my own life force away each time I did it. However, I do remember going along to one particular show where there was an older couple, Colin Thake and his wife Margaret lovely, lovely man. They've both passed over now sadly. He was at the show, and he was deaf. I used to bump into him walking his dog as I walked my dogs. I noticed this one morning that he was limping, and I said, "What's the matter with your leg?"

He told me he was gutted as he was planning to go to the Essex Show that day. Colin always loved tractors. Unfortunately, he'd managed to twist his knee and couldn't go. I asked him where he lived, and I said I'd come over and see him later that morning. I remember he said, "What are you going to do?" So of course, I told him I was a spiritualist medium and a healer. I'm always telling jokes and I used to joke with Colin too. I literally know thousands of jokes and I can tell them till the cows come home. For some reason I've always managed to retain them.

Anyway, apparently, he went home and he told his wife and his daughter, that he'd met this lovely comedian and he's going to pop round and see me later. I shot round there once I'd finished walking my dog Bandit who I had back then. I went to his house which was only 200 yards from my house. I told him and his wife I was going to do some healing and his wife said, "He's not a bloody comedian Colin! He's a medium!" They both laughed as I did some healing on his knee for about 20 minutes. I went off to get something out of my car and as I came back towards his front door, Colin walked straight out of his house towards me. So, I stopped, looking rather puzzled. He said, "I'm now off to the Essex Show!" With that he did a little dance in front of me, saying, "My knee is great!" We became great friends after that. Colin and his wife Margaret always used to give me curry and chips when I went round there. When Nicky and I later moved to France, they stored a lot of our furniture for us. They were such good people.

When I met Albert Lamb, who was also a healer, I gave him a reading and he said you're the best I've ever met, and I've seen a lot. He told me, "There's something wrong with you boy, there's something inside which is tearing you apart." I said to him, "Albert why have they given me this gift? I've been a womaniser and used weapons on people. I've been involved in some heavy stuff in my past."

He said to me, "What do you know about the Governor boy?" I was taken aback and slightly confused so I said, "Who is the Governor?" He said, "Come on boy! The Governor! Jesus Christ!!" I said, "Well I know that he had Disciples."

"Exactly!" he said. "Where do you think he got his Disciples from?" He told me, "No churches. They were from whore houses, docks, bar rooms they were all hard living, swearing, nasty bits of work. They were brawlers and fighters." He said, "Jesus wanted men that he could mould. People that had attitude. People that were strong. People that were loyal." He told me, "You've got all of those qualities. That's why you are going to be very good. You are good now, but you'll get even better, because you're fearless. You'll go where other mediums won't go."

That sort of answered my questions overnight. Then when I read up on the Disciples that is where they all came from. Not that I see myself as a Disciple of course!

*Fact: It is widely reported that Jesus was a different sort of rabbi as he chose his disciples, rather than being chosen by them. Jesus' words are very powerful when he explains that he has come to help the outcasts in society, and not follow religious laws blindly. "Those who are well have no need of a doctor, but those who are sick. I have come to call not the righteous but sinners."
*Source: Mark 1: 16–20 and Mark 2: 13–17

I received this kind testimonial by email I thought I'd share with you. All of the true-life accounts in this book I can back up with the actual emails I've received from the people. I've checked with each of those who have emailed them through to me that they are happy for me to use their experiences in this latest book. Here's Simone …

Where do I possibly start?! Ronnie put a post up on Facebook saying that he'd had a cancellation for a private reading. I jumped on it straight away and got to see him that same morning. He absolutely blew me away with what he picked up. Since that day I have sent my entire family to see Ronnie!

We became friends and he also did some healing on me. Before then I had suffered for years with chronic bladder pain. After each healing session I would come away absolutely buzzing. Ronnie is just the most funniest, kindest man. Handsome as well.

**Lots of love Green Eyes
from Mixamate Concrete**

Whilst I will always be eternally grateful to the Spiritualist Churches for giving me an initial platform. After a while, I pulled away from them. They became too demanding. For example, I'd go from Braintree all the way down to London [almost an hour each way]. I'd have to leave my house about 12 o clock and I wouldn't get back 'til after 6 o clock so the best part of your Sunday was gone. I'd work there and give messages and they'd pay you in £1 coins and 50p pieces, no more than £15 in total. It would barely cover my fuel.

Also, when I was doing the churches, I found each time it was the same people attending. One time I remember, I won't name the venue of course, but it was a type of spiritualist church. I was giving out messages and they had a tea urn at the back of the venue. It was loudly whistling away throughout my readings. As I gave out messages the assembled crowd would get their message and then chat about it while I was trying to give out messages to other people. Then to make matters worse they were also getting up and down, scraping their chairs while they helped themselves to tea and coffee. After I'd been working for an hour, I asked how long they were expecting me to go on for and they had no idea. I never went back there! I think they gave me £20 that day.

Saying that, I've been to other churches where the chairperson in charge has been very good and had a proper format to the afternoon. On those occasions the chairperson has also called people up for chatting over the top of me. Keeping them quiet so that others could receive their messages.

There was one Spiritualist Church which was very different to all the rest and that was Maidstone. Now I also used to do readings for Radio Kent at Maidstone when I was backwards and forwards from our home in France. I'd make time to stop there and do readings for them on the radio over the phonelines for their listeners. At the time, Maidstone Spiritualist Church came up with an idea and I really don't know how it started. Everyone that came in, and because of this thing they did I used to pack the place, despite only earning about £30, it was never a big earner. I didn't mind because it was a nice place to go. It was a long drive, but they came up with the idea of giving everyone a raffle ticket when they arrived. If your number was drawn, all you said to me was who you wanted to speak to, so what their relationship was with you, but no names, nothing like that. They might just say, I'd like to speak to my husband or my wife, or my son, my daughter or my nan.

On this particular day, unbeknown to me, they'd all been praying that this particular fella, I think his name might have been Peter. Everyone was praying that his ticket would come out of the raffle and that he would be the one to get a message. Low and behold his number came out first. I said to him, "Who would you like to speak to Sir?" He told me, "My daughter." That was all. Straight away I said to him, "I have a sense that you've been beating yourself up because this was a weekend passing, a Sunday. I'm being told that your daughter was epileptic and that she actually passed in the bath upstairs and that you and your wife were downstairs watching the TV. She's telling me that you've been beating yourself up thinking could she have made a noise that you missed, or did she scream out and you feel that you should have heard it. You keep thinking could we have done something? She's telling me absolutely not. She had a terrible fit and I'm not sure now if she drowned but the message she gave me that day, it was exceptional. I've only ever done that type of raffle style of reading at that particular church. Some people will say Oh no, you shouldn't be told anything. I can tell you it was very well received. It was a fantastic church run by lovely people. Of course, being on Radio Kent reading for their listeners via their phone lines meant that I had quite a following there. Nowadays I don't go over the water [Thames] anymore. Now that I live in Essex, what with the bridge [QEII Dartford Crossing] and the timings and the traffic I don't work in Kent anymore, but I used to thoroughly enjoy it.

Another spiritualist church which was run really, really well was at Greys. They used to say you can do the hymns in Reggae or whatever you wanted to do. It was really professionally run. I always used to say to the audience, "I don't want to give an address, I just want to do Mediumship." They all used to cheer when I said that. When you'd finished the night, you'd go downstairs, and there'd be sandwiches and cakes and cups of tea. They would have someone there with you to stop anyone coming to talk to you until you'd had a chance to finish your tea and sandwiches. Then that person would say do you mind speaking to someone. People would either want to say thank you for the message or to ask did you see anyone around me? It was a lovely church but again it was in Kent, so I lost a few followers there by stopping. I tend to work in Essex, Suffolk, Cambridgeshire and Hertfordshire only nowadays.

I don't want this book or indeed my first book to be about, 'Look at me, how clever am I' I think there are so many bad mediums out there who sadly can put people off an experience of having a reading for life. I've heard of people who will never go back, and I've also read people who have told me how bad their experiences had been in the past.

Unfortunately, it can be almost comical to watch some so-called mediums. They don't give any proof of what they are saying, and the trouble is then people think that we are all the same. So, with this second book, the reason for my writing it is to put out there just what can be done.

To show that you can actually get a lot of proof from the spirits not just 'Does anyone know a John?' or 'Did he die from an illness?' you know what I'm saying here. You can actually get some really good personal details. I think it's also good for people to hear and read about others' experiences when having a reading. I also think that it's very comforting, especially when someone comes to me who has lost someone to suicide or a sudden heart attack. That person never got the chance to say goodbye. Also, people come to me because there was a family fall out just before the person passed and that matter remains in their minds as unresolved. I can prove that things can still be reconciled.

In my opinion churches should do less events and only use good mediums as there are not enough to go around, instead they can use some very poor ones so they can meet up every week or more.

So, it's for that reason I went over to doing my own shows in restaurants, hotels and golfclubs. I find especially with men, you don't often see men in spiritualist churches. It's nearly all women, but you do get the odd few. But men will come to a restaurant. Even if they don't believe, but their partner does. They will come along for the food and a beer. I worked at a restaurant in Dunmow called Square One for 12 years which was on the High Street. I've done some great work there. It's closed now. It's become something else.

One night I had Mike Reid [English comedian, actor, author and television presenter. He is best known for playing the role of Frank Butcher in the soap EastEnders. He also hosted the children's TV game show Runaround. He was known for his gravelly voice and strong London accent.] come through, little did I know until she raised her hand, but his widow Shirley was in the audience that night.

On a separate night but at that same restaurant, Lenny McLean the bare-knuckle fighter, came through to his daughter. Lenny died in Bexley in 1998. I didn't know it when I started speaking that night, but Lenny's daughter Kelly McLean was in the audience. I remember she was gob smacked because I was able to give his full name straight away.

I've also been working for 14 years with Marconatos in Hoddeston. I can honestly say that the amount of men that come along, mainly because they can eat and drink, and they come along for a laugh. I've had so many of them in tears. They come up to me afterwards and tell me that they thought it was all a load of crap but now they are converted. They say things like, "You're so easy to talk to because you're a proper geeza." Or "You do this but you're a fella?!" I think they turn up thinking they are going to see someone who resembles Doris Stokes. Complete with a perm and a frilly dress! I've lost count of the times I've had the comment, "You're a medium? Really?? You don't look like a medium to me!"

CHAPTER 2

A MOTHER'S LOVE

A lady sent me a message the other day. She said she went to one of my events and knew the message was for her, but she didn't put her hand up. Interestingly I knew on the night that the wrong person was taking the message. I remember that night because the message said that it was for a woman who never finished what she started. It turns out she was a teacher but jacked it in before she qualified fully. I'd said that this lady was also obsessed with frogs. The lady told me that her Mother was obsessed with frogs. It turns out she had ornaments of them and if she found a dead one would bring it home and varnish it! This lady told me that the names I read out and the situations I'd described that night were all absolutely correct.

She wrote in her email, that she wished she'd put her hand up on the night.

That happens every show. I do understand that it can be daunting being at a show and having a message come through to you in front of over 100 other strangers in the room.

Nicky's dad Les, when he was alive was exactly the same. He came to one of my shows once. I gave him a message that night, not knowing it was for him. I said to the audience that night I have a man here called Ted and Nicky was saying to him, Dad it's for you. However, he just sat quiet. His dad was Ted. Nicky knew the details were for her dad, but he just froze. In the end I had to leave it.

Ronnie said he had a lady come through for someone obsessed with frogs. My daughter was the only one in a room of about 85 people to raise her hand.

Ronnie said Mum was into frogs as well as my daughter. We responded, "Well not really, other than some concrete ones around the fishpond, not something she was known for." However, on the way home, it suddenly hit me. My daughter has moved into my mum's home, and there are now frogs everywhere. I think it was Mums way of saying she's seen them. It shows that even if you can't take something at the time, it soon falls into place.

At another reading, Ronnie jokingly called us the Jeremy Kyle family as there was my stepmum, me, my daughter, stepmum, cousin and uncle. He asked my stepmum if she had lost a baby with my dad.

Never one to shy back, Mum [in spirit] said to Ronnie "No that was me!" Ronnie tried to be polite and said perhaps he was with another lady, but Mum persisted telling him. "I know, it's the same man." Ronnie said he was getting the tune in his head of Dualling Banjos and felt it was the record, rather than a reference to a banjo. My dad had it played as the tune his coffin went out to. When he was alive my dad and my uncle used to play it together, so it was very special to him.

My husband is a non-believer but has come to a couple of nights. I have asked him what he thought of other people's readings, and he said he couldn't explain how Ronnie could be so accurate. He said he was also funnier than a lot of today's comedians and his quips and retorts made him chortle.

Tracey White

Clacton-on-Sea

My first connection with Ronnie was also my first time seeing a medium. It was at what used to be called Bensons Bar in Braintree. I had come with someone as support to her after losing her very close friend. I'm not a sceptic but open minded on a very personal level. I lost my Mum when my son was two and I knew she was still around to guide and help. I've felt her sat at the bottom of my bed. I didn't worry as I knew it was her.

So, on that night we were sat on the righthand side at the back of the room, in pitch darkness. Ronnie was talking to a lady who was to our left, and she was frankly, trying to put a square peg in a round hole. Yes, she may be thinking of moving, yes she may move rurally, both Ronnie and her weren't convinced the message was for her. Then Ronnie asked if her mother used to sew, "Ha! My mother never sewed a stitch in her life!" the lady said. However, my mum loved to make our clothes. Then he asked, "Who's Nancy?" I was wearing my Great Aunty Nancy's wedding ring. He carried on, "Why is that ring silver and not gold?" Bearing in mind you couldn't see I even had a ring on. So, I answered him, "Because I have it plated." I said, I still do. Then Ronnie went on to tell me things I'd forgotten about. The house I lived in at the time was rural, my then partner was at the airport, he saw red outfits and a lounge. My son loved being a goalie, he knew we'd sold the blue Merc for a silver family car. Ronnie went on to say my sister is distance away, and that our Mum never saw her son. I've been to a few of his readings since and I have had a private reading too, every time my Mum elbows her way into a reading!

I will say, the last time I had a chance to see Ronnie, I was all ready to go then I realised, I didn't need to go after all. You see, I take so much peace from knowing Mum is still around, and so I decided that this time that my seat could be used by someone else in need of the healing he's given me .Take care Ronnie, stay safe x

Michelle Woodall

Mum is not even stored on my phone!

I will always be indebted to Ronnie for helping me get through the grieving process of losing my mum. He made it so much more comforting knowing she is still with me.

I had a weird thing happen to me the other day in my car whilst driving. My phone rang & (please see pic) I had to pull over!.

That is testimony that she really is with me. I don't even have her stored in my phone!!

So thank you Ronnie because YOU made me believe that she really is, & now she keeps popping up ❤️, *Ronnie, I've never met a medium who is as comforting and accurate as you, you are fab.*

So I first knew Ronnie when he was a bouncer at Kings nightclub. I had my very first reading with him back when he was doing them in Witham, from I believe, it was someone's house who he knew. I came along very nervous, not knowing what to expect, having not been to see a medium for a while. Ronnie made me feel at ease and asked me for a piece of jewellery to hold. From that moment on I was blown away. He began by naming both of my two children, I had at that time. I was going through a very sensitive court case time and he knew that and exactly what it was all about. Ronnie told me all about it and was so accurate. I still have the tape recording to this day!

Alison's mum

I carried on coming to see him for many years after that. Recently I saw Ronnie up in Braintree. I asked if my daughter could sit in with me and listen and he agreed. He made us both cry as my mum came through to my daughter and her messages were such a comfort to us both.

My mum said that my daughter visits a tearoom (which she does) and she knew all about my granddaughter (my mum never met her sadly, but she knew about her).

Along with my daughters, we have visited Ronnie at the Headgate Theatre over the years too. Thank you is never enough for helping us Ronnie, you're an angel.

Take care

Alison

My dear late mum who loved her rich tea biscuits.

Ronnie and I go back a long way. Our paths have crossed so many times. When I read his first book Medium Rare, I realised just how many times we had met over the years.

My daughter and I had private readings with him a few years back and we were both amazed at the things he brought out, a lot of which he would never have known.

One thing which sticks in my mind is my late mother shouting "Biscuits!" When she was alive, she loved her rich tea biscuits and would always say to us "Don't forget the biscuits!"

Bless you dear Ronnie, we shall meet again in the future at some point for another session, I'm sure. Thank you for everything, bless you.

Shirl Waterman xx

My mum and I used to joke about the afterlife and if we were honest with ourselves, never really believed. Having had a transplant at age of 25, my mum used to always say to me, "Don't you leave me!" We made a promise to each other that if there was any truth to the afterlife, we would do whatever we could to reach out, no matter who went first.

We jokingly, made a secret word that we never shared with anyone as it all seems a bit crazy. After losing my mum to Sepsis very suddenly with no warning, I didn't know what to do. I lived with my mum for all of my life and didn't know how to be without her. I used to feel stupid, silently begging her to make me a sign, to let me know she hasn't gone, but nothing ever came.

I didn't know how to be without mum

My husband made contact with Ronnie as a last resort. I wasn't sure about it at all, but I felt I had nothing to lose. I don't want to appear rude, but sometimes I thought Mediumship was a way to prey on the vulnerable but, Oh my! How wrong was I!

He knew me and my mum's word!

Ronnie seemed to already know so much. He immediately knew for example that I was going into mum's room and spraying her perfume before I went to bed.

He asked me if I had any questions so I asked him if he could tell me the secret word that mum and I had.

He told me that it doesn't work like that, but Ronnie held my hand and spoke a sentence. To my amazement, the word was within that sentence! I was buzzing, I just could not believe it. Out of all the words in the world, he knew me and my mum's word!

I cannot thank Ronnie enough, no words are enough to say how he changed me that day! I am now a true believer, and I know she is still with me always.

Thank you, thank you so much

Helen Mouncher

XxX

I remember that it was really strange the week that I had planned to go and see Ronnie. I was going to go and see him in Halstead on the Wednesday, but I was really poorly so sadly I couldn't make it. I was so sad and upset and was thinking about him. At that moment my mum's song came on the radio. I really think that was a sign from her to say, "Don't worry, you don't need a message to know I'm here." Or it could have meant "Jennifer, get your arse over to Halstead now! I want to talk to you!!!"

Anyway, I have lots of stories from my own personal experience and that of friends and family, but I want to share the very first reading Ronnie did for me.

I lost my mum, who was also my best friend, on 29th August 2000. It was very sudden. I talked to her every day and still miss her every day. I remember a close friend saying Ronnie was doing a show (not sure you call it that?) in Halstead around that time. I have had readings before with other clairvoyants/mediums and I'm definitely a huge believer of the afterlife.

I also used to watch Ronnie on telly! I think it was a few days after my mum passed away. I went along and sat in between two friends. He was amazing. We were laughing and crying along with the rest of the audience. He gave readings to many people. Then sadly he said, "I have time for just one more. 'Who has lost someone very recently, like a few days ago"? I excitedly put my hand up with another lady. Ronnie was saying a few things and we both realised the reading was for the other lady. However, he said to me, "Come and see me after."

Ronnie continued with the lady's reading and after the evening had come to a close, I walked over to him with my friends. He asked me to sit down and he said, "I'm sorry but your mum drunk herself to death." I was gobsmacked because that's exactly what had happened. Ronnie continued to give me a lovely personal reading. All of which was spot on. All three of us were crying. If it wasn't for my friends telling me things that he said afterwards, I would have thought I heard what I wanted to hear, meaning he could have said anything. Both friends said it was wonderful of him.

Ronnie, that was and still is, one of the best moments of my life!!! When I went to mum's funeral after that, I knew I wasn't saying goodbye, she is still with me and my family. It helped me to get through the next few days, weeks, months, years. In fact, it still does.

About a month after mum passed. We had a power cut. My two children were asleep in bed and my husband was still not in from work. I got a few candles and lit them. Suddenly I felt a presence. Sadly, I felt scared. I felt as if I looked in a mirror, I would see a spirit, so I kept my head down. Now that I've had time to reflect on that experience I long to see spirits!

A month later I saw Ronnie in a church in Sudbury. I don't think he was 'officially' giving readings that day but suddenly he picked me out saying, "I don't usually do this, but I've got a message for you. It's from your mum." He went on to describe her. Then he said, "She is sorry she scared you. Please don't be afraid of her." Wow! Ronnie that was just brilliant, thank you.

Since then, I have been to many of his shows. I take family and friends. And we always have a good cry as well as a good laugh. Ronnie really is amazing. Thank you.

Last year my family and I went to one of his shows in Earls Colne, Essex. My son-in-law (who was a sceptic) wanted to tag along. My god is he glad he came! Ronnie gave him a reading from his real dad (who he doesn't even call Dad) who had passed away a few months earlier. They weren't really on talking terms and hadn't been for years. However, they we're trying to sort things out, literally months before he passed. The message Ronnie gave was spot on as usual. We were all in tears. My son-in-law always used to listen to my stories after I had seen Ronnie but now it really has made him believe. Again, Ronnie you were/are amazing!!!

Well, I could go on and on about the wonderful readings I've had and how coming away from his shows (even if I don't have a reading) just makes me feel so good and happy. I get signs from mum and my nana all the time. Hearing them talk through Ronnie is just the best.

Jenny xx

My name is Chris and I'm of about the same age as Ronnie. I've worked mostly in construction and engineering all my life so of a particular mindset I would say. I deal day in day out with tangible facts. If it doesn't contain Pi, and I don't mean steak and kidney, then it's not real.

The reading Ronnie gave me, for which I will be forever grateful, changed my life, outlook and belief.

This reading was about March 2019 so five years ago. Let me just say I was a complete non-believer, this was a solid, unshakable thing for me. I always said, "When you are gone, you're gone, end of story. So, make the most of it while you're here." My wife, however, was the complete opposite and to keep her happy we started to attend Ronnie's events held at the Rugby Club near Buckhurst Hill/Loughton in Essex.

Debs my wife would drag along various people and a real bonus for me was a licensed bar so I could at least get a beer during the event.

I did feel for the people there in the audience. Most were looking for some kind of comfort and to witness the pain that some people were reliving during the show was quite hard to deal with. Even though generally, almost all those that received readings were comforted. Comforted in a way. that, at that point, I could not comprehend.

I think it was our third visit to the Rugby Club and I have to say, by that time I had spoken to him after a show, just to ask how he manages to tune out. As I thought the constant contact must be an issue. Which honestly was me saying to him that I was sceptical. However, we had a chat, and I must say he passed my, 'Is he a straight up sort of bloke?' test.

Anyway, our evening progressed as normal, we sat in the middle, next to the aisle on his left, about halfway back. As he appeared to be winding down the show, Ronnie looked straight at me without the normal scouting for a match. He said something like, "I have a lady here" and it went on from there. At the time I was shocked. It was completely unexpected and the most emotional experience I have ever had. Even now years later, it still gets the tears going.

Ronnie had my mum there and what made it so emotional for me was the fact he was coming through with things that were not quite correct but in fact were wrong in only the way my mum used to get them wrong. So in fact he was spot on. How could he possibly know? For example, I did drive buses for a while in the recession in the late 1980s which were 74s out of Camden Town, and Mum always said 78s. Plus she always hated my motorbike and called it a 'bloody scooter' and for a 955i Daytona that's a bit odd. She also used to do the wrist actions [revving the throttle] which he did on stage. There were loads more things he said, and it was joyful to hear. I used to think my relationship with my mum was often volatile, but it forced me to look at things from a different angle.

Mum always hated my motorbike

After the reading I was shocked, so we just left to go home. Usually, I'm the type that would want to come and say thank you and shake his hand but alas I didn't (sorry about that). Later I messaged Ronnie to say thanks and he added something else not said in the public reading. He said that my mum was a really bright and strong woman. He said that a bright light had came through to him at the start of the evening and was next to me, where I was sitting in the audience, the entire time. Ronnie said that he saved it until last as he knew it was going to be special, well it was for me.

Something else which I did not mind, was the comfort that my reading gave to others at the event. Afterwards several people said to us, as we were leaving, what a fantastic reading it had been.

Lastly, I do now think that there is something there (it's made going to the toilet a bit odd!) I now think that we do watch over our loved ones after we pass. It's made my outlook on life just that little bit less scary. So, thank you again.

Kind Regards

Chris Roberts

I lost my mum on the 19th of January 2020 very suddenly. She was a great believer of the spirit world and always went to see Ronnie when he was local doing his medium nights.

On the evening of the 19th, I messaged Ronnie told him I just lost my mum and asked for a reading. He told me he was sorry for my loss but give Mum time to find her way into contact in a couple of months.

I messaged again a couple of months later and he then booked me in for the 15th of April.

I was so nervous but so excited and curious to go. When I arrived, Ronnie put me at ease straight away. I felt calm as we sat in his dining room at the table and he held my hand for a minute and then he started talking.

Ronnie told me so many things that day, and I'm glad I have it on tape to listen to it again and again. At the time I went to go see Ronnie we still weren't sure why Mum passed away so suddenly. The post-mortem had come back inconclusive, and she was only 56. Ronnie told me that it was quick and most probably a blood clot or an aneurysm.

He asked me if my mum had had an operation on her back that had affected her leg and he was correct. She had had an operation on a nerve in her back which had started to send pain to her leg. 18 months later at mum's inquest this was all confirmed.

Ronnie described to me in great detail what my mum was wearing. He told me it was a nice blue top and fancy black leggings and also made reference to what she was wearing on her feet and laughed. This is because we'd put my mum in her slippers.

Mum passed so suddenly

He also described some of the things we had to put into mum's coffin with her. He was going on about a glass bottle but was determined it was not alcohol as some people sometimes do. After a few minutes he said it smelt nice and was a bottle of perfume. He was correct as my sister had put it in with my mum as she bought my mum a new bottle of perfume for Christmas. Every time I went to go see my mum in the chapel of rest the funeral directors sprayed this perfume for when I went in. Ronnie laughed and said, 'But it's not Opium is it? Opium was my mum's favourite perfume but that was not the bottle that was in the coffin with her. So it did make me smile that he knew that.

Ronnie also told me that I had two children, two girls and that they were very close to my mum. This is true as my girls had their own bedroom at my mums and would stay once or twice a week when I was working. During the reading Ronnie did come out with my girls' names, which are Phoebe and Frankie.

Ronnie told me that my mum loved my partner, and she was proud of him but that she was saying to Ronnie that he didn't do my bathroom. I couldn't help but laugh! My husband has a painting and decorating business and had told mum he would get her bathroom done but never actually got round to it.

During this reading, Ronnie kept asking me, "Who is Linda?" At the time, the only person I could think of was my sister's mother-in-law. Her name was Linda, but he kept laughing, saying, 'No, Linda!' It wasn't until I left and listened to the tape again that I realised he was talking about my sister. Me and my mum had a joke and used to call my sister Linda Carter from EastEnders when she *was drunk. I even mentioned this during a reading at my mum's funeral, so this really did make me smile.*

At this the same reading, Ronnie asked me who Jane was and that she was with my mum. Jane was my mum's cousin who had unfortunately passed away before my mum.

He also told me about a man with my mum called Eric. I had no explanation for this man. No knowledge of anyone called Eric when I came home and spoke to family. I was told my mum had an uncle called Eric that had passed.

Now this is a funny one, Ronnie kept telling me that my mum was telling him the name 'Wilma' and laughing. To my knowledge there was no one in my family with the name of Wilma. I couldn't think of anyone with that name, so he left that one with me.

In June as Covid started to settle down we were able to sort out my mum's bungalow. Whilst there one day, when I opened a cupboard in her room, a present fell out. It had a card on it which said, 'To Wilma, love Sally.' I absolutely froze. It wasn't until I spoke to my auntie that she told me that one of my mum's friends nicknames was Wilma.

Ronnie also told me he had someone with him that was close to me. After a few moments, he told me his name was Jeff. Two weeks after my mum we had lost my husband's grandad. His name is Jeff. He said he had connections, overseas and a lorry firm. Ronnie did tell me the name of the lorry firm, which I cannot remember now, but I couldn't make this connection when I left and talked about this with family. It turned out he did have a lorry firm. I spoke to my husband's nan, and she also confirmed the name of the lorry firm, which Ronnie had told me.

There was so much that Ronnie told me in this reading he could just not of known. This gave me so much comfort and peace. After this reading. I did return to Ronnie a couple of months later with my brother and sister, so that they could feel the same peace and comfort that I did. Ronnie told us so much about my mum. As we were leaving on this occasion just as we were about to walk out the door, Ronnie grabbed my hand and said, 'Kelly, who is Toby?' Toby was one of my best friends that I had lost four months after my mum. Ronnie told me he was now with my mum, which once again gave me great comfort.

I've since seen Ronnie a few times at his medium nights and am always so amazed at what he does and says. I will be forever grateful to him for letting me know my mum is at peace and that there is life after death.

Thanks

Kelly Robertson

It would be an honour for my mum to be mentioned in this book as she was one of Ronnies' biggest fans. Me and my mum (Carole) had been coming to see Ronnie for over 20 years [at his public events where there are many people] and I had never had anyone come through to me.

Sadly, mum was unwell and so she made me a promise in her final days that if I needed to go and see Ronnie at the first opportunity I could, she promised me she would come through. And didn't she just !!

Mum Carole with daughter Paula Purvis

Ronnie came straight over to me saying my dad's name (Brian) and how he likes everything tidy and in order and my brother's name (Trevor). Ronnie was able to tell me what was wrong with mum. Also, her best friend's name (Mary). He talked about her Irish roots, her nursing career and how mum was the sort of person who would give you her last £10 if you needed it.

More comforting to me was my two daughters (Sydny and Georgia) were with me and Ronnie turned to Georgia and told her that she was wearing mums ring and there was a stone missing from it which there was!!

My mum was our absolute world.

This meant the world to me and my girls. My mum was our absolute world, and it broke us all when she passed away.

Ronnie's message proved everything. I had been brought up to believe and it has helped us to move on. Knowing she is ok and out of pain.

Paula Purvis

This is my story.....

My story starts on 4th December 2014, I was getting ready to go out on the town for a Christmas work party, I was late as usual leaving. I got a call from my mum's partner saying he was unable to wake my mum up, my initial thoughts were, he always overreacts, but I could hear the fear in his voice, so I called my colleagues and told them that I would be late as I would have to detour to my mum's house some 30 minutes' drive away.

On my arrival I found my mum in bed upstairs, her partner stated she had been feeling unwell today and took herself to bed in the afternoon. She was unconscious but rousable to a degree, but something was not right. An ambulance was called. Once in hospital and many hours later my mum was rushed for life saving surgery, she had suffered a sub–Cranial Haemorrhage. Basically, she had brain aneurysms that had ruptured, causing blood to swell around her brain.

She was placed in Neuro Intensive Care. I remember talking to the consultants about her condition. He said think of your mum's life as an orange cut into quarters. With your mum's condition, a quarter do not make it and die at home before they are found, a quarter die on the way to hospital, a quarter make it to hospital but the damage done by the bleed is not reversible and they are left in a vegetative state and the last quarter walk out of here with some effect but can learn to adapt to the disabilities they have been left with.

He stated your mum is strong to have made it this far, we now have to sit and wait. She had been placed into a coma, so her body could try and recover.

This was the beginning of my life changing as well as hers. The roller coaster of a ride I had just boarded.

Days turned into weeks, I never left the hospital for the first three weeks, after only returning home for a few hours before returning after that. Sleeping on chairs, sitting by her bedside for hours on end. Machines alarming, tubes and drains everywhere, my mum lifeless.

My mum had woken up

Three weeks later on a Sunday afternoon, I had a call from the hospital to say that my mum had woken up. Oh my God I cried and cried. Mum had to have more surgeries and after seven weeks was transferred to the High Dependency Unit at the hospital. The consultant said to me,

"Your mum is strong and has beaten the third quarter of the orange." This meant everything to me, but what the future held no one knew.

For the next 17 weeks she remained in HDU. She was unable to walk, eat, drink, dress herself, use the toilet, she needed total care, and she hated this. She was frustrated with herself and as a family and in particular me. I used to get the full barrel of her frustrations. We have to remember before this brain injury she was a totally independent 64-year lady who lived life to the full. She also now needed oxygen all the time.

In June of 2015, she was medically fit for discharge, but with her care needs, it was decided that she should go into a intensive rehabilitation unit. I remember on the first day I made a deal with her. She loved to holiday in Turkey and would go at least twice a year. She wanted to go back to Turkey in September 2015. This was a long way from where we were currently, but my deal was, you need to work hard and push yourself to your limits then we'll get you back there.

On the 3rd of September she was on a plane to Turkey albeit with a portable travel oxygen cylinder.

In December 2015 Mum got married to her partner. When covid hit, my mum had difficulty in understanding why I could not come around and why I could not take her out. No matter how many times I told her, she could not retain this information. I spoke to her daily, Facetimed her, but it was not the same.

At the end of June 2020 she was hit with pneumonia. On the 4th July 2020 we received the call from the hospital to go to the ward as mum had taken a turn for the worse. I remember driving there to meet my stepdad outside and I had a sense that I was too late. I had a feeling that she had already gone. I can't explain how or why, it was just a sense that I had. We were shown to a relative's room, which just made this feeling I had even stronger. We were told she had passed away peacefully, and the rest was a bit of a blur. My stepdad was in bits. I remember asking if she was still on the ward and that I would like to see her. At this point I broke down. We spent about an hour with her and the guilt I felt that day was devastating.

All I could think about was that she was all alone. She didn't understand that it was not my choice to not be there and that it was the restrictions that were holding me back. The grief was unbearable.

On the 28th of July I messaged Ronnie privately, the feeling of guilt I just could not shake. The whole experience had me devastated. Both losing my mum of course, but the sense of her thinking we did not care, we did not visit. This part was the worst. Before then, all that she went through, I was always by her side, except this time when it mattered the most.

I had always believed there was an afterlife of some kind and I had attended one of Ronnie's shows previously. I felt for the people that had someone come through with him that night and remember thinking then how spot on he appeared to be. One of my friends had also had a previous 1-1 with Ronnie and she said that I should contact him. She could see I was struggling.

I kept up with Ronnie's Facebook notices. His private readings had such a long waiting list and had to be closed on many occasions due to the sheer volume of people wanting readings by him.

I decided that I needed to try to get a reading. At this point, I would have travelled anywhere, I was so desperate. I knew I had to see Ronnie. I had the sense he was special. He gave readings with so much accuracy, he gave names and dates. I read his previous messages left on

Facebook by other people, plus my friend's experiences. I had been to previous readings with other mediums and maybe the cynic in me could see how they were not giving names, but in some ways trying to guess, or cleverly getting the person to reveal the answers.

I sent the message to Ronnie asking to be considered for any cancellations and gave a small amount of information.

All I put was that she passed away in Covid, and that I haven't seen her in months due to the restrictions. To be honest I was not expecting an answer back, as I knew his list was closed currently. The following afternoon I received a message back. Initially Ronnie was telling me off! He said that I should never tell a medium stuff. He told me they should be able to tell you. He gave me an offer of a private reading for about six weeks later. I grabbed the opportunity in both hands.

On the day of the reading, I was nervous and excited all rolled up in one. I had felt mum was around me and I talked to her when I was alone. I told her I was seeing a medium today and had a question that I needed answering. I told her I still feel guilty all the time that I was not there for her.

My question that I wanted answered was, Did she now know the reason why I did not visit on her last hospital admission? Does she now realise that it was not a choice I could make? That it was out of my hands? I kept this thought to myself and did not tell anyone.

Ronnie greeted me at the door, and we went into a room with a table, I sat one side and Ronnie the other. He recorded the session with my consent. My mum came straight through, he described her to a tee, *and he was spelling out her name. Mum was showing him, letter by letter until he got it. That gave me the clarification I needed to know it was her, but it did not stop there.*

He was shown an American flag flying. Ronnie asked me why the flag is being shown, but my brain did not click at that immediate time. My mum had no connections to America at all. Then it came to me, my mum passed on 4th July 2020 American Independence Day. Ronnie told me that she was in hospital and there were issues with her chest. She had COPD. He knew about her oxygen. This all gave me further clarification.

I listened to him intensely. He then said that she is telling me not to feel guilty and that she understands. This is what I had been waiting for. At that moment a great weight lifted from me. The stress and guilt I had been feeling just fell away. It's so hard to describe that moment, I came to Ronnie because of the sense of guilt I felt for not being there, but it was like the mist that had hung over me had dispersed.

The reading went on with Ronnie talking about my children, getting their names, even explaining about my son whose name is Jordan, but I call him Jay. Then they came to my youngest Kira who was heavily pregnant when my mum passed away, she never got to see her great granddaughter. Ronnie said that mum has seen Robyn, this gave me so much joy. Robyn was born three weeks later. It made me think about the times when I have had Robyn and she always seem to look in a corner of the room where no one was. She just looks there and smiles and giggles to herself. Like she knew someone was there watching over her.

Ronnie continued, telling me how proud mum was of me. This gave me such a feeling of warmth. I always felt I could do more and had not done enough. My theory of life is there is always one child that steps up and is the organiser, the helper, the one that does more. In my line of work I see it time and time again, so I am that one person everyone relies on.

My mum also said to Ronnie that she had fond memories of a place, something with Cherry in the title. This I could not place, but took it on board to ask the family at a later time. I did indeed ask the family and it was a place her siblings went to Cherry Lane when they were growing up. She spoke about her brother Dave who had also passed. All this gave me further clarification that this was her. No one could know all these details with such accuracy. Some things I didn't even know about!

Ronnie was finishing his reading with my mum. He said that she is okay where she is, she was so tired before, she is in no pain. Ronnie explained that all the conditions have gone, any pain has gone, she is at peace.

I will be forever thankful to Ronnie to give me this opportunity. I know that he is in high demand. I don't know if he could sense my desperation in my initial message, but this was how I felt. This cloud continued to follow me every day, it consumed me when my mum passed. Having this reading with Ronnie lifted this cloud, allowed me to believe that my mum is in a better place. She battled for a long time and gave everything she had and if anyone deserved a rest it was her.

I will be and I am, eternally grateful to Ronnie, for his time and his reading when I needed it the most. He will never know how much this meant to me.

Forever thankful

Sharon Lockey

CHAPTER 3

FATHERS

My dad Ronald Gordon Snr. passed away when I was 44, he was only 66. I have seen the spirit of my dad, only briefly, he looked like a much younger man when he came through to me as all of the spirits do. Only our physical body ages. Here are some of the readings where I've encountered other people's dads ....

I first attended a group meeting at Finchingfield village hall in July 2016. I went with my best friend as we had both lost our fathers around 13 years ago and we were hoping for either of them to come through. The place was rammed, and Ronnie had a very busy night as lots of people came through. It was right near the end of the night, and we had kind of lost hope that we would get a reading. Just as Ronnie was finishing up something came through. It took him a little while to figure out what it was, and I remember Ronnie said it was very rare this happens. We all waited in anticipation, and he finally said aloud it was a horse! The whole room started laughing and my best mate and I just looked at each other in amazement as my dad and I rescued a horse together and she died not long after dad passed. Ronnie started to describe this horse it's colour and markings and it was indeed our horse! Then he asked if anyone recognised this horse to put their hand up. So, I did. Ronnie's next words were that a man was standing next to this horse. He went on to describe what this man looked like and what he was wearing. He had a beard, glasses and was wearing a hat and wore cowboy type clothes. It was absolutely spot on for my dad!

Next Ronnie started laughing to himself, he went on to tell us my dad had just got on the horse and fell straight off the other side! This was always a joke with my dad and I. He always wanted to ride our horse but said if he tried, he was sure he'd fall off the other side! Well, it had finally happened!

Ronnie then started to wiggle his thumb and said to me, "Your dad is doing this, and he says it's all okay now." This was because my dad was a carpenter and one time, I was working with him and he very nearly cut his whole thumb off on a bandsaw! My dad also told Ronnie to say that he was all good now and not ill anymore. Ronnie knew my dad died from throat and stomach cancer at the age of 50. I hadn't said anything about this at all.

Ronnie went on to say that my dad was asking about some people and one of the names was Charlie. She was the girl that used to help us look after our horse. Dad told Ronnie about the scars I have on my knees. This was from when I had an accident on my moped. Dad wasn't happy about it still (not my fault by the way!)

Then a dog appeared! Ronnie knew the breed as an Alsatian and even said his name 'Prince.' This was our family dog of 14 years, and he was absolutely spot on again. The reading ended by my dad saying to Ronnie that he is always watching over me and loves me dearly.

It was an absolutely amazing, mind-blowing experience and a fantastic end to the night. There's no way on earth Ronnie would have known any of those details. It brought me great comfort and belief to know that my dad is happy, well again and with our family pets. I went on to have a private reading with Ronnie and once again I was absolutely blown away with the detail. Some things I'd forgotten myself!

I would love to go back for a third reading with Ronnie as my life has certainly changed in the last four years. I absolutely know now that it's been my dad guiding me to get me to where I am today and that's been with massive help from Ronnie. There's most definitely life after death.

Take care

Sarah Pope x

I came to Ronnie's house for a private reading, too scared to drive, so I took the train from Romford. He made me feel at ease the moment I walked in, sat me down, and we had a little friendly chat first, then took my hands for a connection.

One of the first things Ronnie said was that I'd looked after my mum during her illness and that I was wearing her ring whilst he pointed directly at the very ring (I was wearing five rings at the time). He said I was with her at her passing. Then he mentioned my dad, saying he had a leg injury during WW2, but never spoke of it, I knew nothing of this, so dismissed it. On the way home, thinking about it, I realised he'd been knocked down by a car in later life and eventually lost his leg.

When I came to one of Ronnie's shows at Harold Wood, my dad came through – he had him to a tee, his rank in the Army, his "funny" ways. Ronnie described him exactly!

After the one-to-one reading, I felt great comfort, a wonderful calmness and peace inside, I thank you Ronnie.

Regards, Viv Rowe xx

I was first recommended to Ronnie back in 2016, when I was in serious need of comfort after losing a few loved ones. I was at a point in my life where I couldn't see the point of living any more without them. My friend told me to pop Ronnie a message to get on his waiting list. It was the 4th of November 2016 when I had my first experience with Ronnie. My dad had passed away 14 years prior to that. I'm not kidding you when I say I felt like I had the first conversation with my dad in 14 years! Ronnie described my dad exactly how he looked, even touching his right ear saying my dad had his ear pierced in that ear. He described his horse tattoo on his chest. He told me things no one else in this world would know, apart from me and another of my passed over loved ones.

For example: There was always a joke between me and my friend before she died about spoons. When we were younger, she used to think you check if pasta was cooked by putting a spoon on top of the pasta. She thought if it bounced out from underneath the pasta then it wasn't cooked. Ronnie told me she was laughing about the spoons! I couldn't believe my ears!

I literally could write pages about my first ever reading with Ronnie. He even picked up my friend Richard who passed in a car accident and told me his nick name. He told me in two years I would have another baby. As I was driving to Ronnie's that day, I was such an anxious wreck. I even took a friend in my car for support.

When I came out, she couldn't believe the difference in me. My whole attitude to life in general had changed. I felt so comforted and blessed to have had that session with Ronnie. I literally felt like my kids had their mummy back. My anxiety had calmed down hugely. All I needed was a genuine chat with my dad through Ronnie. Just to know him and my other loved ones were all ok.

After that first reading with Ronnie, I dragged my friends to his open sessions and everyone fell in love with him. I love watching the comfort that Ronnie brings to people's lives. My second reading was on the 28th of March. I was even more speechless than the first time! I walked into the room and sat down, and the first thing Ronnie told me was "Your dad's here and his telling me you're expecting a baby!" I was only five weeks pregnant! I couldn't believe it! Throughout that reading I got even more comfort from lost loved ones. The whole reading completely blew me away.

Exactly two years (all bar three days) of my first reading on the 4th November, our beautiful little baby Tommie was born on the 1st

November. Ronnie was once again absolutely spot on! I have no words to express how much comfort this man has brought to my life. After years of therapy in just a few sessions with Ronnie and I literally feel like he's saved me.

Thank you so much Ronnie, I cannot wait to see you again one day.

Sherri Gray(Sherri Ann)

Ps sorry it's so long, I had so much more to say but your book would be full of just my review!

My first-time seeing Ronnie was at his home in Braintree for a private reading in 1999. The first thing he said to me was that I have a Greek Cypriot Father/Grandfather figure in the spirit world. Ronnie went on to say that I also have siblings in Cyprus and that I would one day meet them.

In 2021 my children brought me an Ancestry DNA kit as a present. I did the test and the results revealed that I am in fact half Greek Cypriot. This led to me asking my mum for the truth as I'd grown up thinking that someone else was my biological father. Even though we never had a great bond, and I went years without seeing him, he was known as Dad. He married my mum in 1969 and she became pregnant with my brother. They were all posted to Famagusta in Cyprus with the army where my brother was born. My mum and 'Dad' made friends with a local Greek married couple who they met at a dance who had a two-year-old daughter.

When my brother was christened, this couple were my brother's godparents. Little did I know my brother's godfather would turn out to be my biological father. My mum and 'Dad' moved back to the UK with my brother, and she was already six months pregnant with me.

My mum and 'Dad' separated and eventually divorced. There were questions over the years as to why I looked so different to my brother. He's very fair yet I'm dark with curly hair.

Going back to 2021, curiosity got the better of me and I needed to find out about my Cypriot Father and siblings. It took me two years and eventually in January 2023 I found, and made contact with, my Cypriot half-sister. She was shocked but never doubted me for one minute. I decided to get a next-day sibling test to be doubly sure and the results were that we are indeed half siblings. My half-sister now lives in Scotland with her family. She has been estranged from her parents for 36 years (we also have two brothers also that reside in Cyprus).

For obvious reasons I've decided not to make contact with my biological father in Cyprus. I'm now 53 years old, and it would only cause upset as he and his wife are elderly and not in great health. Since January 2023 I have spoken to my sister every day (often more than once a day!) We have visited each other with our families and are booked to go to Cyprus in May with her husband and my partner.

Having a sister in my life is more than I could have dreamed of back in 2021. My brother-in-law, niece and nephew are the 'icing on the cake.' My four children have gained the loveliest aunt, uncle and cousins, and my granddaughter has gained a great aunt, uncle and great cousins.

Last year in June 2023, I saw Ronnie again. He mentioned that I would be going over to Cyprus (my brother-in-law booked it at the end of August that same year.)

My emotions at the time of my first reading with Ronnie were shock, when he said these things to me. Although I do remember back when I was 16, in 1986, my mum's friend (who was also posted to Famagusta with her serving husband) told me there was no way my dad was my real dad. At that time no one would confirm it. It was always in the back of my mind. When I saw Ronnie, I was even more convinced but couldn't think of a way to ever find out for sure.

It wasn't until my four children got me the Ancestry DNA kit that I knew the truth one hundred percent. I felt excited and at peace if that makes sense. DNA doesn't lie. It never mattered to me that my mum had a relationship with another man. I understand these things happen be it right or wrong. I just wanted to know the truth and I eventually got it. My mum is also now happy for me that it all worked out.

I can say that from the time I got my Ancestry DNA results in May 2021, it was an emotional two years for me. I did find cousins who gave me information about my Cypriot side of the family.

When I saw Ronnie again last June he also got my Cypriot brothers name right ...I have the recording still ...no way would he come up with a name randomly like that.

Donna Landells xx

The very first time we saw Ronnie was in Braintree and he mentioned my wife's father John and said he had drowned in either Cyprus or Greece, this was true, it happened in Halkidiki. He also mentioned that we had two children and that a third was 'waiting should we want another!' Well, not so long afterwards we were blessed with our second daughter Harriet who is now 11.

Pat's first husband and Lisa's Dad John

I offered Ronnie a drink afterwards at the bar and he had a pint of orange squash and said that John was still in the room. He told me John was a lovely man and is always around my wife and her Mother Pat which was very comforting. We have recently come back from our first visit to Halkidiki and organised a boat trip out to the spot of the accident and laid some flowers down in his memory with Harriet. It brought some closure after all these years for my wife who could finally find peace and say goodbye to her dad.

After this visit it was a few years before seeing Ronnie again but what happened on this night was simply unbelievable! Scroll forward in our lives to the 6th of October 2017 at a spiritualist evening hosted by Ronnie in Witham, Essex. Ronnie had a message from a man who died in a car accident with his friend, this turned out to be my wife's cousin. Both names given were 100% accurate, along with details of the location. My wife had only recently discovered that her cousin had died. The family had fallen out but, due to her uncle's last wishes before he died, had recently reconciled.

Next, Ronnie got my wife's dad coming through again (John). He mentioned our children, my son's name being very similar and that he was named after John and my brother. We named my son Jack which is what the Irish call John and his middle name is William which was my brother's name.

He also mentioned that my wife's mum (Pat) had remarried, that it had happened quickly after she lost her husband (John). Ronnie said that John knew her new husband before his passing, all of which were true. They used to play bowls together!

Ronnie went on to mention a song by Matt Monro - 'Softly as I leave you'. We couldn't make any connection to this on the night but said we would see if we could find any connections to it. My wife took her Mum shopping the next day and mentioned the messages from last night over a cup of tea. Pat (my wife's mum) opened her purse and handed Lisa a piece of paper with the words written on it – 'Matt Munro, Softly as I leave you' and a date on it from over four years previous. Pat had put this in her purse way back then, as this is the song she wants played at her funeral!! When the wife told me over the phone, my jaw nearly hit the floor!

Thank you, Ronnie, for all of your messages, we've seen you a few times now and each time has been an amazing experience.

All the very best,

Rob & Lisa Phelps

I came to see Ronnie with a couple of friends at one of his shows in Roxwell, in Essex. I can honestly say that I really didn't believe in it all, but I was intrigued. I wanted to come along to see what he did now. I'd met Ronnie once or twice in the 'good old days' when he worked on the doors with my brother.

I can honestly say I was blown away that night. Even though nothing came through for me, the people that had messages were mind blowing. I came away with a totally different view and straight away I booked for a private reading.

I had to wait a while as he was so busy. Eventually the day came when it was my turn. I came in, still a little uncertain, and thought to myself, 'I'm not giving anything away'. Well, was I shocked! First, he put me at ease and then as the messages came through, I couldn't believe it. My dad came through, he died when I was 17. I was with him at the end and Ronnie told me what he said to me. No one else knows that because I've never told anyone! He also told me how my *dad had passed and that he didn't want me blaming myself anymore. I had for all those years blamed myself. Ronnie told me that my dad is with me all the time watching over me.*

There were other things too at that same reading. My brother and my nephew came through as well. However, I will never forget what Ronnie said about my dad and it certainly changed my thinking. He truly is gifted, and I can't thank him enough.

Carol Carter

I've seen Ron quite a few times in group settings. I would say my most memorable reading was my one-to-one reading with him. I went to his house which is very welcoming. He read me and said he is out to prove there is life after death. He told me lots of things that stunned me even though I'm a believer. I was shocked by the things he was telling me. The thing that stays in my mind the most is when Ronnie said about my dad. He told me, "He has a warm and caring energy and he had literally turned up with a folder full of things, as if to say let's prove this to her!" That's exactly what my dad would do!

Emma's Dad

Straight away Ronnie said, "What's the lightning tree?" My mouth fell open!

There's no way Ron would know about the lightning tree. It's the tree from my childhood. My cousin and I built a tree house in my garden, after the tree had been struck by lightning. I could relate with everything Ron had said in my one-to-one, apart from just one thing. He said to me, "You have a new friend Billy and your Dad says you're to have your wits about you with regards to him as he is not very nice." A week later a family member also warned me to stay clear of Billy. They told me he was not to be trusted. I stepped back from Billy at this point, after these warnings. The following month Billy got arrested and is now inside!

Thanks for looking out for me Ron.

Luv

Emma

I've had many messages and a few private sittings with Ronnie, but this message is the most poignant of all to me. I wanted to share one of my messages from back in 2011, when I saw Ronnie at Witham Public Hall.

Months after Dad's passing, my sister and I decided to pay a visit to Ronnie at one of the local village halls. Little did we know, our encounter would be filled with astonishing connections and comforting revelations. As Ronnie inquired

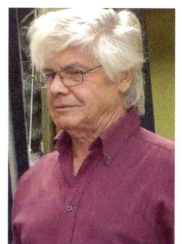

Dad's pride in her shone through

about Dad's watch, which my sister happened to be wearing that evening, he mentioned Frank, one of Dad's pallbearers. What truly astounded me was Ronnie's insight into our lives. With his hands held like an open book, he spoke of Lily, my 8-year-old daughter, and her touching tribute at Dad's funeral. Dad's pride in her shone through his words.

Memories flooded back of Dad's bedtime stories, lovingly shared with the grandchildren told from his hands as if Ronnie were Dad standing in front of us holding a book. Through Ronnie's messages, we found solace in knowing that Dad still watches over us, and that life transcends the boundaries of death, offering us reassurance in our grief.

Mandy x

CHAPTER 4

PETS

I often get asked about whether animals pass onto the spirit world. I can say that most definitely yes, they do. I get asked about the loss of pets all the time. Pets can literally be a lifeline for many people, especially as they get older or live alone for whatever reason.

Although I hear about them from the spirit people who have passed on, I have actually seen horses, dogs and cats in the spirit world. So yes, rest assured your pets do go to the other side of life. They are looked after by people who have gone before you. So, if you have lost a mum or dad or a loved one, they look after your pets when they pass. Then when it comes to your time you will see your pets again when you cross over. We all know that our pets are like very close members of our own family. I mentioned that I had lost several pets including my beloved dog Bandit. He was a Staffordshire Bull Terrier and we lost him in 2014.

I've actually seen him very, very clearly since he passed. I could see him one day right in front of me, he was literally standing there wagging his tail looking up at me.

I have seen our French cat Aubert (pronounced Albere), in spirit. He had only one eye and was the smallest cat you've ever seen. Saying that he was ferocious, vicious and a nasty piece of work but a beautiful looking cat who swiped many a person who came for readings!

Aubert our one-eyed French cat

I've not so far seen my other dog Bella, who we rescued when we lived in France. She passed in 2020. She was a lovely old girl, meant to be a Pitbull terrier but she wasn't. She was just a big ol' lump of a dog!

Bella was a big muscular dog but with a very small head. Anyway, in her earlier life she'd been mistreated and so she had a bad disposition. Despite that, we took her home and we loved her. It took a couple of years, but Bella became the most beautiful dog. All the people who came to me for a reading when Bella was alive would remember her. She always greeted everyone with a waggy tail. She really was a lovely old thing.

It was 2019 and Bella was just approaching 15 years of age. I remember taking her out in the morning and she was like a puppy again, running around, playing and happy as could be. I remember I commented to my wife Nicky about how well she'd been walking and how lively she'd been. When we got home, Nicky went off to work and I did what I had to do, some readings, I think, that day.

Anyway, about five o clock that night I was about to take Bella out for a walk, as I was booked to do an event at the Town Hall in Maldon, that evening. I went to take Bella out and she was laying down rather like a Sphynx would lay on her belly with her head up.

I called her, saying come on Bell, time for walks. Nothing. She just lay there in the same position. She had her back to me so I was looking at the back of her head and she wouldn't even turn her head to look at me. I walked round to the front of her and her eyes were wide open but she was just staring. I lay down next to her and waved my hands in front of her face and still nothing. She wouldn't even blink. Just staring straight ahead, still breathing but just not responding to me in anyway. I knew at that moment that there was something badly wrong with Bella. I continued to lay next to her, gently stroking her. There was still no reaction from her. About 5.30pm that night Nicky came in from

My beloved Bella

work and also my stepdaughter Amy. I called them both over straight away and I said, "Look there's something seriously wrong with Bell."

They said they'd have to book her in at the vets, but I said, "No, you need to take her in now!"

I couldn't take her as you can't have people travel miles to see you for a reading and then let a room full of people down at the last minute. Plus, I knew there'd be people there who needed messages so you can't just not turn up. Therefore, Nicky and Amy agreed to take her. I picked Bella up, cuddled her and carried her out to the car and I laid her on the back seat. She was very passive, just laid there. Her big yellow eyes just looking straight ahead. I kissed her and stroked her head and said, "Come on Bell, you'll be ok." I had to watch as Nicky and Amy drove off to the vets.

In the meantime, I got ready and went off to the show at Maldon. I was worried sick, and I had an inkling that I'd never get to see Bella again on the physical side of life. I certainly didn't want to think that, but that's what came to me. Anyway, I got to Maldon and did the show and managed to put it right to the back of my mind. I came out about 9.30pm and I went straight to the car parked around the corner and I phoned home. Straight away when Nicky answered the phone, I could hear that she was crying, and I knew the worst. She said, "I'm so sorry Ron, she's gone. I had to let her go, I'm so sorry." I told her, "Nick, its ok, I understand, I'll be home soon." I put the phone down, sat in my car and in truth, I probably cried for 20 minutes that night. I just sobbed. I knew I'd see her again at some point in the afterlife, but I so loved this dog, and I missed her silly ways. I still miss walking her of a night after a show. I miss coming home to see the look she would give me and the wag of her tail. She had a good life, and she had a long life but she was still like one of my kids.

When I got home that night Nicky was in bits. She kept apologising to me and I kept reassuring her it was ok, I understood. Nicky told me that when she'd got Bella to the vets and the vet had said it was something like a seizure or a stroke. The vet had said that Bella was in a lot of discomfort even though she wasn't showing it. They said to Nicky that the kindest thing to do was to put her to sleep there and then. Nicky had said as it was my dog was there any way they could wait until I finished the show that night. The vet said as she was extremely unwell and also uncomfortable if it was their dog they wouldn't drag it out. She was just lying there and was really cold, so they'd had to put these little blue socks on her to try to help to raise her body temperature. So, Nicky did the right thing saying ok let her go. Nicky and Amy both loved Bella as much as I did. They were beside themselves. I'd like to have been there for her at the very end. Nicky saved me the pain of seeing Bella looking so ill at the very end of her life. I never did see her physical remains as she was cremated. She's now buried in the garden along with Bandit.

A year later in 2020, we lost our cat, the famous Aubert (pronounced Albere), he was a wonderful cat. I've still got videos and photographs of him. He would walk down the street with me and the two dogs. He would walk beside them like a little dog. Aubert was so savvy he wouldn't go near the road, instead he would walk through people's front gardens. He would stay close to me and only cross the road when I crossed the road. He was a real old soul and he lived till he was 15. One day, all of a sudden, he started crying all of the time. He was also being messy which he never was before.

One night we saw on Facebook someone had posted, that there was a one eyed cat sitting in the road. Aubert had only one eye and previously he would have never done that. We immediately got in touch with the person who posted. Now no one could touch Aubert, he wouldn't let anyone go near him. He was feral and he was a wild cat. Basically, he was a vicious little bastard!

He was beautiful and I loved him but he would even turn on me sometimes. He didn't like strangers and he wasn't in the least bit scared of dogs either. He would have a stand-off against any dog.

However, these people who had posted about him being in the road managed to pick him up and put him in a box and they brought him home to us, but sadly he went downhill from then. Now Aubert was a tiny little cat with one eye but feisty as they come. We rescued him during our time living in France. We got Aubert at the same time that we got Bella. However, it was Aubert who dominated the house. Nicky and Amy were the only people who could do what they wanted with him. He frightened me and both the dogs! If Aubert was sat in the doorway and the dogs were outside, they would not attempt to try to come in the house past him. They would sit out in the garden and wait for me to move him. Sometimes I'd have to call Nicky to move him! That's just how he was. You had to catch him in the right mood, but I loved him all the same.

On the day we had to take him to the vets we took him into this little room. Nicky held him and cuddled him and he just lay there. The vet gave him the injection to put him to sleep and told us he'd gone. Nicky said, "He hasn't he's still breathing." The vet said to us, "He's gone I gave him a big shot." Nicky still protested and said, "He's still here!" So, the vet checked him and he said, "Oh my god you're right!" So, he had to give him a second injection. Even with the two injections he lasted for another couple of minutes that day. The vet couldn't believe how strong this little cat was.

He was also cremated, and he's buried in our back garden as well. Each of our pets have their own plaques. I still walk down the garden and say good morning to them or goodnight and chat with them. I know they are still around us. I've since seen the spirit of Bandit very clearly. I've also seen Aubert in the side of my eye, in my peripheral vision. I've so far never seen Bell, but I do know when she's around me.

Michelle Clements came to me for a reading and immediately I could see the spirit of a horse, a grey horse. I told her you've lost your horse and she started to cry. As the images came to me, I could see pictures of Greece and, as I've been there before myself, I recognised where in Greece they were.

Michelle said to me, "I bet you can't tell me the name of my horse." I told her Zante as that's what I could see in my mind. She was blown away, that was indeed the horse's name.

However, Michelle was still sceptical. Now I like to do a bit of metal detecting in my spare time and Michelle has 10 acres of land. So, I asked her if she'd mind if I did some metal detecting on her land. I do it just to find old bits of jewellery and relics from the past as I can also do psychometry [reading facts or impressions about a person or thing received through contact with an object that used to belong to another]. I used to buy jewellery from secondhand shops when I was first honing the skill. I've got, for example, an American university ring that I know comes from a man who fought in Vietnam and lived to be an older man. I could tell that just by holding the ring.

Zante was indeed the name of her horse

Michelle on her horse Zante

I've kept that ring because it has a lovely vibration to it and that's what I do.

Michelle lives in an old cottage, which is timber-framed and from the Victorian era.

They've also had a house built on some of the land which is beautiful. They are a lovely family with dogs and kids. Michelle said I could go where I wanted and do what I wanted.

All I did find there were old horseshoes, a few nails and a spoon!

While I was there Michelle said they were planning to knock down the old cottage which stood on the site to make way for a home gym. She told me she thought that the cottage was haunted and asked if I'd mind taking a look.

I stepped inside the cottage with my son-in-law David. I told Michelle, yes you have got a spirit here but it's one of a lovely, lovely old lady. I think her name is Betty. I continued to tell Michelle that Betty was a spinster and so never had any children of her own. I told her, "Your bedroom is at that end of the house, and you have a Sunday morning ritual where the dogs and the kids will be on the bed with you and you have tea and biscuits." I said, "Betty watches you because she didn't have any kids of her own and she loves your dogs too. She's telling me that she had a brother whose name was John, and he was a local vicar and

Betty used to play the organ. She was here until around the 1920's."

Michelle said she'd have a look at the local parish records to do some research. Michelle was true to her word and messaged me a couple of weeks later. She wrote,

You got everything exactly right Ronnie, other than the old lady's name. Her name was actually Miss Pettitt. She did indeed play the organ and lived in the parish as a spinster. Her brother was the local vicar and his name was John.

Michelle went onto say, she always thought that perhaps I was a mind-reader and that's how I did my readings. She said, in her message,

How could you tell me things that even I don't know?

Here's Michelle talking about that reading in her own words

I met Ronnie many years ago for a reading. I was very sceptical but went anyway. I hadn't imagined him to look like he did to be honest.

What does a medium look like? He was handsome and very muscly!

Anyway, what he came out with astonished me! He said my horse's name was Zante. Well Zante was not and is still not a common name for a horse. I was shocked! He also said I had a Staffie and Jack Russell which I did and that I lived on a farm which again I did.

That reading was years ago, fast forward to a year or so ago so probably 2023 when I had another reading with Ronnie. He told me

that my nan was called Margaret and was crying. My nan was advising me to not speak to my mother named Kay. Again, these names were true, and he could never have known them. My mother is a horrid woman, and I was brought up by my grandparents and I have not spoken to my mother in many years.

In the summer of 2023 Ronnie popped over to my old cottage that was soon to be knocked down for my newly built house, he wanted to do some metal detecting. Ronnie told me that an old lady named Betty visits me in the evenings and sits on my bed and that she likes me. He said that she was barren and some connection with the St John's and that she was a stout lady with glasses and her hair in bun.

I was speaking to a lady in our village about what Ronnie had told me. I was so shocked when she confirmed there was a Miss Pettitt who lived in this cottage many years ago and donated the organ to the St John's church in Mount Bures village.

I have always been sceptical, but I can sincerely say that Ronnie could never have known any of what he told me, he sure has a gift. A lovely open, honest man that I have had the great pleasure to meet.

Michelle Clements

When we saw Ronnie, he got a dog of ours come through. He said it was a crossbreed but definitely part German Shepherd. He said he was a bit confused as the person with the dog kept saying he wasn't a proper dog. Ronnie said that he could see it definitely was a real dog.

Not a proper dog

The reason for that was the person with him was my late son-in-law and he used to play with the dog and tell him 'he wasn't a proper dog' as he had one ear that stood up and one that flopped over.

He always used to laugh at the dog and say that he was broken.

Lorraine Atkinson

Not a pet as such. Ronnie told me, in one of my readings, with him that I would be moving. To which I said no. Then he said there would be a link to frogs. I didn't think much more of it. Until a couple of years later I had to move due to a change in circumstances to the house where I am in now.

Every time we have heavy rain, the lawn in the back garden gets lots of frogs jumping over it! We don't even have a pond!! I still don't have any idea where they have come from. Just one of many things Ronnie has said to me over the years that have come true.

Thank you, Natalie

Millie 2007-2022

I came to Ronnie for a private reading, in September 2023. I have always loved the idea and believed in another world. However, as this was my first private reading, I went in hoping and wishing from signs on this side of life. I was not expecting anything though to avoid disappointment.

Well Ronnie, you literally blew me away within the first 30 seconds! He took my hand for the link and one of the first things he said to me was, "Who's Millie or Mollie?" He also knew straight away that she was a terrier. My dog was called Millie and a Yorkshire cross Norfolk Terrier. The reading then diverted elsewhere to various family members and friends that have passed over. Next Ronnie went back to there being a photo of someone wearing tartan and I said no it's definitely not my kind of pattern to wear, or my nans. Ronnie wouldn't let it go. He kept getting the message to go back to this and the spirit wouldn't let this go so he persisted and went back to them for guidance. He told me that there is a tartan blanket, which is red and the spirit world was showing him a picture of this. I was so adamant about this not being for me.

Who's Millie?

My final goodbye to Millie

Then the penny dropped, July 2022 we cremated Millie in her bed. What went in with her inside the bed, was her favourite sausage toy, with her grey jumper on, wrapped in a fluffy red blanket and she was placed on top of a grey, white and red tartan blanket.

When I said my final goodbye to Millie on this side of life, I decided to take one last picture of her.

I knew this was my last chance and I could always delete it if I ever changed my mind. I was very aware I wouldn't get this moment back, so I took it.

I have never ever shown anyone this picture before, let alone shared it on any kind of social media.

It absolutely blows my mind that at some point, whether that be the spirit who was in the room that day, with me and her, before she went in and I was saying goodbye to her, or that the spirit world has been looking over my shoulder at my phone on the rare occasions that I have revisited that picture in sorrow - at most twice a year.

There is no explanation as to why Ronnie knows what he does, and he has completely changed my outlook on life. When the going gets tough, I know that there are spirits behind me, listening and watching beside me and he has proved this to me. In my opinion, people that are sceptics but never take the chance to come to a show and see, are narrow minded and undeserving of being graced with Ronnies priceless gift.

I love everything about mediumship, spiritualism and look at this in the happiest light there can be. It has truly turned into a hobby of mine to come to shows and I'm in awe of the other side of life and how powerful it is.

There is no amount of money I wouldn't pay, to give back what you have given me Ronnie and I sincerely thank you for that.

Kind Regards,

Olivia.

Back in 2020 not long after I lost my husband, my daughter and family came to see Ronnie at one of his evening shows. What he said to us that night was amazing. Ronnie told me so much about my late husband but the main thing that stuck in my head and proved to me that it was him was when he mentioned about a white rabbit. This made me think, how would he have put a man and a rabbit together as it is pretty rare.

My neighbour's young daughter had two pet rabbits that used to escape regularly. One didn't make it unfortunately, but this other white rabbit became wild and took a liking to our garden and stayed living freely for roughly three more years. It literally used to eat, sleep and live in our garden and my husband and I used to look out for it and feed it every day. My husband was very fond of it and loved this rabbit and it used to put a smile on his face whenever he saw it.

My husband took a liking to the rabbit

Animals in general were a big part of my husband's life and it makes sense that Ronnie would pick up on a story like this when making contact with him.

It's these personal touches in his readings that keep me and my family coming back to see Ronnie over and over again. He is also always so down to earth and genuine and has given me some emotional and unforgettable experiences over the years. What he does with his readings has brought a small measure of peace and comfort to me after the loss of my husband and I know many of my family and friends feel the same about his readings.

I have attached a photo of the rabbit for you to see. Thanks again for all the amazing readings. I could go on and on with how bang on and to the point Ronnie has been in them.

Best of wishes,

Sharon Webb

XX

For the past eight or maybe nine years I've been invited along to the Danaher Animal Home in Wethersfield*as their guest of honour at their open days. There is usually also Radio Essex there and they have stalls. They invite people to come back who have rehomed rescue dogs from them. I open the day and I let them raffle off one of my readings via a silent auction. I do it every year and I also take an RSPCA collection box round to all of my shows as the Danaher Animal Home is affiliated to the RSPCA. So far, I've raised £18,500 for them.

The Danaher Animal Home is a big part of my life.

They also always ask me to judge Best Rescue Dog on the day and every dog has got their own story. Some were really badly treated and when I hear about each of them, I get very emotional, and I end up in tears on the day.

I stand there and I have 30 dogs and only five rosettes to give away. I always end up apologising to all the other dog owners who don't win. The Danaher Animal Home is a big part of my life.

*The Danaher Animal Home is a registered charity based in Wethersfield on the Essex and Suffolk border, set on 5 acres of land. They have over 45 dedicated staff members within the organisation and a large volunteer network who work hard to support them. Each year they take in hundreds of lost, abandoned or ill-treated animals and whilst affiliated to the RSPCA, the Danaher Animal Home is an independent charity entirely responsible for raising its own funds. *Source: www.danaheranimalhome.org.uk/

CHAPTER 5

LOSING MY OWN LOVED ONES

Since the publication of my first book *Medium Rare* in 2016, an awful lot has happened in my life. Some things which for me were very, very sad but also some great stuff as well. One of the saddest for me was the passing of Monique, my niece. My brother Paul and his wife Anne's daughter.

Monique-Lianne Buckingham

08/12/1995 - 03/11/2022

Instagram

@thelifeofmique @the_daily_tobes

With every passing moment we close our eyes, we search for your smile and you are there, Within our minds, within our hearts, we feel you breathe, we hear your voice and hear your song, our beautiful angel you have not gone...Dedicated to our beautiful and courageous daughter Monique who inspired so many to be strong, to be humble and to be the best version anyone can possibly be. Monique's journey began at the age of around 18, suffering stomach pain that doctors constantly put down to IBS. In January 2017 at the age of 21 she was rushed to hospital in excruciating pain. That night her bowel had perforated, and an emergency operation took place revealing that she had stage iv terminal bowel cancer. Two weeks or so prior to that, Monique had been to her GP with concerns that she may have cancer, again showing photographs of blood in her poo. Once again, the GP dismissed her fears and prescribed Buscopan. Throughout her illness,

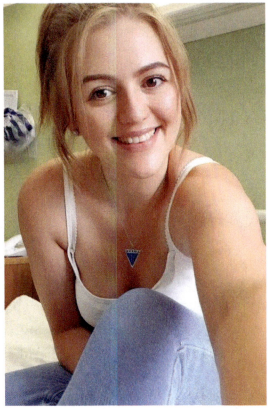

Monique-Lianne Buckingham

she dedicated her time to bringing public awareness to Bowel Cancer and to the Bowel Cancer community in the hope that, in her words 'no one would ever have to suffer as she had and that if she could help save even only one life it would be the greatest gift of all.' Early diagnosis saves lives. For those less fortunate either diagnosed too late or, as in Monique's case, mis-diagnosed, she decided to document her journey with the hope that her Instagram page would help to ease the anxieties, fears and emotions that cancer creates. By keeping her page raw and true, by showing her own vulnerability, suffering and strength to endure the impossible, she did accomplish her dream.

On several occasions, she was contacted by many who had sought medical help after having read her blogs and finding themselves relating to her symptoms. Her most precious and humble moment was the day when she herself was an inpatient accompanied by her little companion Toby, a lady, a complete stranger approached her and simply said ' Excuse me, are you Monique?

'Today is your best life, be free little minions, be free' - quote Monique

I recognised you by your dog Toby. I just wanted to thank you for saving my life. I have been diagnosed with early-stage Bowel Cancer. I would not have got checked out had I not been following you on Instagram' Monique's world suddenly shone like a ray of sunshine as though the lights had suddenly been switched on and all her pain and suffering lifted. Beyond her frailty her eyes gleamed, her smile more glamorous than Hollywood's elite, she had indeed received the greatest gift of all.

That ray of sunshine has become our hope and our knowledge that Monique's life and death was not in vain, she tried to live her best life and encouraged those around her to do the same, From climbing mountains to watching simple sunsets. Monique was and still is our special angel of positivity. Her smile will always light our way...

'Today is your best life, be free little minions, be free' - quote Monique

She was such a brave girl. She's been gone just over a year ago now back in November 2022. It was such a terrible thing for us all. Such a sad, sad time.

Another sad loss was that of my father-in-law Les Jones, Nicky's late father, who passed almost six years ago. He was a lovely man. A 74-year-old kid! Les was the most humble, non-argumentative man I've ever met in my life. He was a complete kid, from start to end. He was never ill. The doctors didn't have a single file on him. The man actually had no medical record, all of his life until the day he fell over and badly broke his wrist. He also developed some other health issues which led to heart failure and sadly we lost him.

He also loved family barbecues and after food and a good drink out would come the bows and arrows and catapults which were aimed at targets all over the garden, much to my mother-in-law's distress! He loved firework night too.

Les misbehaving as he was told not to touch anything!

Les was the most harmless, nicest, gentlest man I've ever met.

He was a real old-fashioned cockney and would talk in rhyming slang. My mother-in-law Pam lives next door to me and Les passed there. All of his boys were there, holding his hand. Pam said to me, "Come on in Ronnie, he loves you too, come in and hold his hand." He was only a few hours away from death at that point. I said to Les, "This doesn't mean I fancy you."

He opened his eyes and looked straight at me saying, "You always fucking say that!" He was at death's door, but he still had that rapport.

Les was the most harmless, nicest, gentlest man I've ever met.

When he was alive Les also loved anything to do with water. So, surfboards, windsurfing, paragliding off the back of a speedboat. Les was also a great swimmer and diver. Les always had a thing about the Vikings as funnily enough, I do myself. He always said he wanted to be cremated in a Viking ship when his time came.

Of course that couldn't happen. When he was cremated at his funeral there was a massive turnout. Literally 100s of people attended. The boys, his brothers, my wife and myself all decided that we would build a Viking ship and put his ashes inside it. Then we'd launch it and set light to the ship we'd built.

At one point there was all sorts of crazy ideas which went along with it including trying to fire flaming arrows at the ship! This of course couldn't happen either.

Anyway, years and years earlier Les and his family had a caravan in Steeple Bay, which is near Burham sort of way in Essex. So, we all went down there, the wife, the three boys, Pam, his widow and myself. We'd made him this small Viking ship which we took to the caravan park next to the sea. We all stood there at the water's edge. We put firelighters in the Viking ship and Les's ashes too. Now Les had always also said, "I can't be burnt, I won't burn." Let me tell you – he was bloody right!

We'd made him this small Viking ship

Eventually we managed to light this boat up and pushed Les out to sea.

However, the boat didn't seem to want to go anywhere, it kept hugging the shoreline.

We had managed to get the boat on fire and there was a good blaze going. Dan, the second eldest boy, he got his paddleboard out and paddled out and pushed the burning boat out with him. He took the boat 30 yards out off from the beach where we were all standing. The boat was still ablaze and showed no signs of sinking anytime soon. In the end we had to manually sink it! I just know in my heart of hearts that Les would have been watching over the proceedings that day and absolutely loving it.

This man always had the most wicked, wicked sense of humour. Les was as funny as they come. He was always the last man standing and he was a very lovable man, I loved him dearly. He would do anything for anyone. Get shopping in for the old ladies up the street. Life was always just one funny thing for him.

Now Les worked as a lagger, so he would go insulating pipes and things like that. He was known on the building sites for being an absolute comedian. Anyway, him and some of his work mates started playing darts at a local pub when they finished work at night. Les made a set of darts that were maybe four or five foot long. So that when he next turned up for darts, he stood on the oche and pushed them into the board from where he was standing to make them all laugh. That's just one example of the sort of silly things Les would come up with. Another time he took some paper cups and glued them onto the back of hard hats when people were wearing them, so they'd be walking about oblivious to the fact they had a silly cup, stuck upside down on the back of their heads!

I also have it on good authority that he worked at Admiralty House, Buckingham Palace, galleries and museums and all of them have the words '*Les Jones woz ere*' scribbled somewhere! I can definitely say that Les is still very well remembered and well loved.

Next came the passing of my own brother Michael, he was 78. That was just late last year (2023). It was only about a year after we lost Monique. I looked up to Michael. He was my half-brother but to me he was always my brother.

Me, my brothers Michael, Alan, Lee and my mum in front

Michael left his wife Jean, married for 56 years, behind and his only son Lee. I always looked up to Michael big time. He was totally different to me. Michael was a straight goer, never got in fights. Very, very intelligent and also very good-looking man. Lovely blond hair which he kept right up until he passed. He had big blue eyes and people would say he looked like the actor Nigel Havers.

Michael was one of the youngest people ever to pass the Knowledge. [Introduced in 1865, the Knowledge requires taxi drivers to memorise thousands of roads and routes within a six-mile radius of Charing Cross, including a range of popular destinations from hospitals and nightclubs to monuments and theatres.] Anyway, he passed and became a London black cab driver. The stories he used to tell me!

He was a cab driver in the early '60s. He drove so many celebrities around including professional footballer Georgie Best, crooner Matt Monroe and musician from the rock band the Kinks, Ray Davies and comedians Bob Monkhouse and Bernard Manning. All were in the back of his cab at some point and often several times. The actor Omar Sharif tried to pull him! My brother was blond with big blue eyes and so a very pretty boy. Omar got into his cab and kept asking him to go here and there and then invited him in for a drink. My brother had to tell him he was flattered because of who he was, but he told Omar, "I've got a wife and a young son and I'm straight."

Me (Left) and my brothers Paul, Lee, Alan and Michael and the little boy in front if Jordon, Lee's son with my mum.

My brother retired to Spain and was a great golfer and would play all over the world. He came home from walking his dogs one day and said to his wife that he felt tired. She was surprised because he was never tired. He ended up going to the hospital and they diagnosed cancer. They found a secondary tumour but sadly not the first one. I visited him on the Saturday, and by the Monday he'd caught pneumonia and died. I'd been in and out of prison and been a bouncer and a ruffian, my brother wasn't like that at all. I'd been married and was divorced, and he'd married his childhood sweetheart Jean and was with her until he died.

I said a few words at Michael's funeral, but I lost it, yes I'm not ashamed to say. I broke down because I loved him dearly.

I'm going to miss him and his chats and his wisdom. He was the best man at my wedding. Him and Jean had moved to Spain, so I hadn't seen a lot of Michael prior to his passing.

Just before he died, he complained of being a bit breathless. That was strange for Michael as although he wasn't a fitness fanatic or body builder like me, he did walk a lot, always had his dogs and he was a very good golfer. When he became ill, his son Lee managed to bring him home and get him into Southend hospital. When I went to visit him on the Saturday he could hardly speak. He had an oxygen mask on. His eyes did light up when he saw me. I sat and held his hand for a long time and chatted to him that day. He looked up to me too in some ways. He always saw me as the tough guy. We always used to laugh together about how big my arms were and the things I got up to. Michael never put me down, he was a good brother. I do know that he's safe and I know that he's still around and now out of pain.

I've also lost a few mates which I worked the doors with. You might remember if you've read my first book *Medium Rare* that I worked the doors for many years. I've lost both Big Tim and Johnny Ham, plus also Pete Spencer, Shaun Spooner, and Kevin Keeshan.

In fact, I could name a few that have since passed over. On the plus side I've also got back in touch with a few of them too. Ronnie Downs and Colin (Bolshie) and, if you 've read my first book you'll remember me talking about Roy Stuart the 6ft 5ins Jamaican, my 'brother from a different mother'. He lives in Tenerife. I'm also still in touch with Kieran White and Scott Grey and also Peter Townswell and Paul Smith (Smut) too.

In my first book I mentioned Paul Stanley he was a firm friend who I met when I was 10 years old in Leytonstone 'til I was about 16. I saw him a couple of times in my 20s and then we lost contact. I knew he hadn't passed as I couldn't feel his spirit around me.

Then on Facebook one day up popped Memories of Leytonstone. So, I posted on there, 'Does anyone know a Paul Stanley?' I added to the post, 'It's quite a common name but we have another mutual friend called Adrian De'ath'. Now that is a more unusual name, so I put that name in as well and within minutes Adrian's wife replied, 'Yes, they're all now living in Clacton.' I couldn't believe it, that was crazy. I'd spent so much time working the doors in

Clacton over the years. I even went out with a girl from there for a period of time.

We'd probably passed each other in the street and never even realised it. Adrian's wife kindly passed on Paul's phone number. Now bearing in mind I'd not seen this man for 30 odd years, or maybe even 40+ years I rang him up and said, "You alright you old bastard?!"

Straight away, without hesitation he said, "Hello Ron!" So, I'm happy to report that Paul is now back in my life again, which is a great thing. In fact, we had him round here for dinner only the other day. He's done well for himself. He's had his own company over the years, and he's retired now. Married with kids, a daughter and sons that I never knew. Now we are in constant touch with each other, which is lovely. It's been so nice to get this friendship back as we really were inseparable for years.

When Paul and I were kids and living in Leytonstone, I always remember Paul's sister Collette being really, really, really pretty. However, at that age I still thought an erection was for weeing over high walls!

Scroll forward 60+ years and Paul brought Collette to see me in 2023. She is still stunning looking and older than Paul and I gave her a reading. She was very pleased with it as she's a very spiritual girl too.

Another great friend that I made in my 20s was Dave Kinnane and at that time I was a 'ducker and diver.' Selling shirts and God knows what else I used to pick up. Basically, overruns from people. I remember this day I cold-called this florists in Hainault. I spoke to Elsa, his mum and I gelled with Elsa and also with Dave. After that we had some great times together playing golf – well him playing and me trying to play! I also knew his girlfriend Tracey, a lovely girl. However again, through circumstances and moving away, Dave and I lost contact which was a shame as he was a great fella and we were great friends with good stories we could share.

I remember one in particular, where he and I went to Edinburgh to watch the golf. Now going back on this story, Dave was an only child, and his mum Elsa was a character! She loved him dearly and she didn't want him to fly, she was terrified of him flying. So, Dave said we'd fly up there, but he said, "Don't tell me mum! Say that you're driving." Therefore, in the florist's shop Elsa said, "You alright Ronnie? You are driving, yes? You swear to me that you are driving." So now I'm on the spot because I don't like lying to her. I couldn't drop Dave in it else we wouldn't have got there so reluctantly I said, "No it's ok I'm driving. We'll drive carefully and we won't go fast."

Off we went and when we were there, we had a good time. During the day we'd watch the golf and at night, we were young men, we'd suit and boot and we went out to see the sights of Edinburgh. This particular night, we came out and stopped a taxi driver to ask where there was some nightlife. The taxi driver told us he knew just the place which was outside of Edinburgh I think. It was in Stenhousemuir possibly? I can still remember I was in a beige two-piece suit and Dave was in a navy-blue suit, always an immaculate man was Dave. Anyway, the taxi driver took us round to this club and I remember looking and having second thoughts, but the taxi driver assured us we'd be alright here.

We paid him and got out of the cab and off he went. We walked up to the doormen, two of them with loads of scars on their faces, who said, "Ah yew lads in ther reet place?!" in a broad Scottish accent. We stepped inside to find that it was actually a working men's club for the local miners!

Everyone but us was dressed in hobnail boots and jeans. The women in there looked tougher than us! Let alone the men. Undeterred we went up to the bar and ordered a drink. You could feel the daggers staring at you. Dave said, "I think we'd better get out of here a bit lively like. This ain't gonna go well for us." But I said, "No fuck 'em, I'm gonna have another drink. We've come all this way and paid for a cab." Looking around the club as we drank, there was nothing worth pulling. It was a really rough and ready place.

We got our second drink and halfway through it the doorman came up to us and said, "Lads, please go, we're going to have to rescue you in a minute because they are not taking kindly to you coming here in your nice suits." So, we swaggered out as best we could with our heads up and jumped into another cab saying, "Thank fuck for that!" We've never stopped laughing about that night and I've still got the entry tickets somewhere too.

Dave and I were there to watch the open in St Andrews the year that [Nick] Faldo won it. One day after we'd got back home again, in the shop Dave let slip to his mum that we'd flown there. His mum went ballistic! She looked at me really cross and said, "Do you know what? The one thing I hate is liars." I remember my heart sank at that moment as she was such a lovely woman and I felt I'd let her down. Then she followed it up by saying, "But I hate grasses worse, so you're forgiven. Especially as you did bring my son back here in one piece!"

Dave's got two fantastic sons, Junior (young David), he has represented England in water skiing. He's able to do trick stuff going over wooden slides, on the water and up into the air. His other son Sam is a really good golfer. He was playing at a golf course in Danbury and I did a show there.

Well Sam, his son, saw the poster with my name on it and said to his dad, "Didn't you once know a Ronnie Buckingham, back in the day?" Anyway, thanks to that, Dave is now back in my life too and we often go out with Tracey, who is now his wife and Nicky my wife. We were even invited when Dave and his wife renewed their wedding vows. Lovely to have him back in my life, another really, really good friend.

Another friend I mentioned in *Medium Rare* back in the '80s when I was having it tough, a man who bailed me out and helped me out all along the way financially was Micky Tingey and we're still great mates. We like to go out every now and then and have a steak together. We also speak on the phone often. I also have a friend, another ex-doorman called John Carrell who I am also still in touch with and we often go out for a bite to eat together.

When I look at my life, I'm really quite a complex character. As you'll see from my shows on stage giving messages, and down the gym, I'm a very loud, witty and confident person. However, in my private life I'm actually very, very quiet. I don't like going to pubs and I really don't like parties. If I'm at a party, I'm the one sitting in the corner. That is just how I am. My wife Nicky's family are all party goers. They all love to have a drink, and they are all musical. Her brother Robert is in several bands. He had a really successful band called "Missing Andy" Les, my late father-in-law and my mother-in-law Pam, would turn up at nearly all of his gigs. It was Les's pride and joy to watch his son perform, even into the early hours of the morning. Robert can play guitar and writes his own songs. He plays drums and piano too. He's very gifted. Her brother Dan can also play a tiny bit of piano and he's a good trumpeter and is a very good singer.

He's probably got the better voice of all of them. Nicky, as I've said further on in this book in Chapter 9, she loves to dance. She'll happily dance the whole night away and she's a very good dancer. Her mum likes to drink, and to dance and as a family they are very outgoing people. Nicky's brother Brian he'll also get up and dance, drink and he'll party till the early hours of the morning. In fact, I call them the Von Trapps!

They know me, I'll get to about 10 o' clock when they are all partying and I'll just disappear into the other room and watch the TV. They all know it's not offensive to them, it's just I like the quiet life. I suppose really, having all those years on the doors, being surrounded by people, especially when I was always working New Year's Eve and Christmas Eve and of course every Friday and Saturday night. Plus, also performing on stage, giving messages on so many evenings. The reality is I'm actually quite a quiet soul.

Anyway, let's take you back to some more stories of friends of mine. To be honest with you, because I do spiritual work and I know a lot of spiritual, nice people I still like people who are rough and ready round the edges. It's always been like that. All of my life-long friends, all the fellas I've mentioned earlier that I train with down the gym are rough and ready people. What I'm saying here is that I still take to those sort of people. A very good friend of mine who I have asked his permission to put this in the book is a man I've met later in my life and his name is Andy Bade. I call him Badie and he's quite a successful man. He used to drive a nice Bentley. He comes out of Manor Park and knows a lot of people who I knew, and we became friends. He came to my shows and Andy went on to become a pretty decent healer himself. He's now moved away to Suffolk with his wife Wendy, but we're still very good friends. Me and Badie owned motorbikes at the same time.

Me and Andy Bade aka Badie

He's also the most caring person, but he's had a funny old life. The man is multi-talented. He can spray and repair cars, he's a mechanic, he can do building work, he's a plumber, electrician. Basically, there's nothing the man can't do. He also makes things out of wood to a very high standard. He is really, very, very gifted. When I bought my motorbike, he bought an old bike, resprayed it and reconditioned the engine.

We always went out riding together and we had some really great times.

The sense of freedom you get on a motorbike is something else. We'd go off all around the country lanes riding together. We'd stop off at tea rooms and have a cup of tea.

When I had my first knee operation I couldn't drive for a long while, so Andy kindly volunteered to drive me. We were driving along one night after a show, and he was telling me that his late mum had been agoraphobic. He told me that he rarely went out when he was a baby because she just couldn't stand going outside. I sat there in silence listening to him tell me about his childhood. All of a sudden, I said to him, "Andy I've got your mum coming through." He said, "You're Joking!" I said, "No, seriously she's here mate. She's telling me that she's very sorry that she lied about the agoraphobia." He looked confused saying, "What do you mean, lied about it?"

I said, "She's telling me that it was actually just because you were such an ugly, fucking baby that she never wanted to take you out in public! In fact, she used to feed you with a catapult!" Well, his face. He did laugh. It was so funny. He called me a fucking, saucy, bastard!

Anyway, a couple of minutes later, he was still driving me home at this point. I told him to take the next left hand turning. He turns into a layby! I said, "Not the fucking layby, the next turning mate!"

I count myself as quite a lucky person. As a non-swimmer, I could have drowned in my younger years – twice!! First, I fell into a duck pond and then later I fell into the Thames.

I was once in a car crash where I wrote a car off. I've also been in some dangerous situations when working on the doors in the past and in villainy too where it could have gone nasty. Thankfully, I've survived them all.

However, this particular time Andy, who is also a very, very caring man, he would always let me go in front when we rode our motorbikes. He always wanted to make sure I was ok. He would always be riding 50 yards behind me. We were out riding one lovely, sunny day riding along the little back lanes on the outskirts of Finchingfield, in Essex. I remember we were coming down this road, it was the middle of the summer. All the leaves were green and glossy on the trees and all the hedges were very thick and overgrown. We came to a blind bend on a road we didn't know. I could see it was going to be a nasty bend, so I slowed right down to about 30 – 35 mph.

Badie was about 50 yards behind me. As I came round this corner, stuck right in the middle of the road, literally taking up the whole road was a combine harvester. You couldn't see it as you approached and then suddenly it was there moving slowly towards me.

Now I'm no Barry Sheen. I can ride a motorbike but I'm not a great motorcyclist. I couldn't have stopped. There was no way on earth I could do it. All there was, was a tiny grass verge which was about 18 inches wide then the ditch. I threw the bike left and right and I actually managed to ride along the grass verge. Now if you'd have given me a hundred goes at it, I would never have been able to do it again. I was inches away from the combine harvester, riding alongside it. Certainly, no more than six inches away from the side of this massive vehicle. The side of it was almost brushing my leg.

Next thing I knew, I'd come past it and was riding behind it. Badie had stopped, he'd had time to stop being that bit further back from me. At this point the combine stopped too. Poor Andy was white as a sheet. When the combine moved on and Andy and I were back alongside each other he said to me, "For fuck's sake mate! I thought that was it for you. How on earth did you do that?!!" I just laughed and said, "Fucked if I know Badie!"

Another story involving Badie which also shows what a kind man he is. I was doing some shows and with this new knee it took a long, long while. In fact, it never really went well and so I've had to have it redone again recently. Anyway, in the early days after the operation I'd still do my shows, but I was I suppose, quite disabled really. I couldn't walk very well. I was out of balance, and I walked with a bad limp. There was a couple of shows that I did, where I'd parked in a multistorey car park. One in particular always had druggies on the staircase, always asking you for a few quid.

When I'm fit and well, even at 69/70 I don't give a fuck, you know. If someone is going to attack me, they're gonna come unstuck. I'm still confident in myself and I've fought many fights over the years and lived in that world in my past, so I'm not worried. To be honest I'd normally treat the person to a few quid, depending on the situation.

But at this point during my knee surgery recovery I said to Badie, "I'm really nervous about this because if I'm attacked and get knocked over, with my knee, I just can't get up. So, I'd get a kicking."

Now bearing in mind that wherever I do a show, I take my RSPCA pot with me. Now normal people wouldn't bother to have a go but druggies and desperate people, they would try and take it. So, I'm aware of that. I've not been a petty thief, but I know what it's about. So, at this point in my life, I really did feel vulnerable.

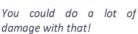

The next thing I know Badie turns up. He's made me a walking stick for me with a metal skull's head on it. He said to me, "There you go mate, you're allowed to carry a walking stick, but the other end is some sort of weapon.

You could do a lot of damage with that!

So, if you are attacked you could do a lot of damage with that."

You could too! I've kept it and I've used it a few times to walk with. The fact that I'm here, and not in prison tells you that no one did try to take the RSPCA pot from me!

Another very good friend of mine, who has been a friend for many years, is an ex-paratrooper called Andy Reid. Reidy is a first-class carpenter and he's now living in France. He moved out there when we moved out there and he's stayed out there all this time. He's had no wives or kids, just a few girlfriends. He's a bit of a disaster in that area! But a staunch mate and the most direct man I've ever met in my entire life. Bang! That's how he is, what you see is what you get with Reidy and no holds barred.

Like myself, he's always lived in the gym, he's out running, he lifts weights and he's had a few gyms of his own.

He bought a big lockup, like a hanger, in Latchingdon near Maldon, in Essex where he used to live. He made his own gym equipment. He made his own leg press machine, squat racks, amazing. He could also weld, do all the carpentry and padded things out. It was a fantastic gym. Sadly Reidy just wasn't a businessman. He was just too abrupt, too short with people. Don't get me wrong, he liked people, if you went there and trained hard. I would let myself in and out of his gym as he gave me my own key. I used to train there every day.

As a lifelong friend I understand Reidy like no one else. We were all in there, training one night and on the walls are pictures of Arnold Schwarzenegger, and Tom Platz and all the big body builders of the day. As you're all aspiring to try to look like them. There was probably about 20 of us in there all training away. All of a sudden, this skinny fella comes in. Tattoo on his neck, had a bit of a swagger with him as he come in. I thought, "Oh here we go!" This fella says, "Who's in charge here?" Reidy pulled a face at me as if to say, this is going to go well. Reidy says, "I am, what can I do for you mate?" The skinny guys says, "Well I want to do a bit of training, get meself a little bit fit and build a little bit of muscle." Reidy says to him, "Ok." But then the skinny guy, he points to Arnold Schwarzenegger and he says, "But I don't want to end up like that." The whole gym went silent. I thought, "Fucking hell, here we go."

Reidy's grabbed him by the fucking throat, pulled him towards him and called him a "Skinny, gutted bastard!"

He told him, "Do you know how hard you've got to train, how much you've got to eat, how much you've got to know, and how much you've got to rest, just to even begin to look like one of them. All of us, we've been training here for years, and we can't get anywhere near that. You don't want to look like one of them? Get outta my fucking gym!" With that he frog-marched this fella to the door, kicked him up the arse and slammed the door shut!

I said to him, "Another satisfied customer Reidy?" He said, "I'd rather shut the fucking gym then entertain people like that." But that's Reidy for you.

There's another story I recall with Andy Reid and I'm already laughing as I remember it. In the old days, whenever my then wife threw me out or something happened, I always had a room at Reidy's house in Maldon, halfway up the hill there. When I had flats, Reidy always had a key. Therefore, if he got himself into a romantic crisis or chucked out, or whatever happened, there was always a room for him at mine. That's the sort of mates we've been and still are. In fact, I'm planning on going out to France to see him again soon.

Anyway, Reidy jogs up the hill, he's a big runner and a big cyclist, typical para. He came back with this watch that does your pulse rate, heartbeat. It's an all-talking watch. This one time, I'm sitting watching him and he's trying to set this watch. Won't look at the instructions, he's just going to work it out for himself. I can see he's getting really pissed off with it. Now without a word of a lie, he's had this brand-new watch for a half hour.

He's effing and blinding and shaking this watch, thrown the instructions away. He's really getting angry now so I said, "Reidy, just jog back up to the shop, it'll take you two minutes and you can ask the man to explain it to you." Then next thing I know, he's gone to his toolbox, got a club hammer out, and he's gone outside. I thought I've got to watch this. Out in his little yard he's put this watch down and he's smashed the life out of it with this hammer. This brand-new watch he's now just completely belted and belted it. He looks over at me as if to say, "Don't you say anything!"

As he's come by me, I've looked at the watch and I've noticed that there's still a little red light that's still bleeping. It reminded me of the Terminator. So, I said, "Here Reidy look that watch is still alive mate." With that, he went back outside, and smashed it again and threw it over the fence, saying, "It's fucking dead now!" Of course, about half an hour later when he'd calmed down again, he said, "Do you know what? I wish I'd taken that watch back up the hill to the shop to ask." But that is Andy Reid.

On that same note it's very, very interesting how you can never judge a book by its cover. When he ran another gym in Witham behind the Swan pub. there was an old fella, called Peter, who used to come in there. He was very lean and spoke with an American accent, although he was English as he'd lived out in the States for years. He'd had four wives and four divorces or so he told us, and he always had good advice about women for us. How to treat them. He would tell us to have fuck all to do with them apart from the sex part.

He always told us, don't marry them and be your own man. It's fair to say he used to make us laugh as he was such a character. He was telling us one day that he had an Opal mine and that he made quite a bit of money from that in the States. He would tell us that he dug opals and made some jewellery from them. Then he went on to tell us that he'd been one of the top TT Rider Champions in America, riding motorbikes. That he'd won lots of trophies and had the laurels around his neck and all that. He told us what a good motorbike rider he was back in the day, maybe in the

1930's. This was back in 1977 when he was telling us this and he seemed to us to be in his 80s then.

He wasn't being flash he just said it as it was. Then he went onto tell us that his son was a world champion kickboxer. So, we were all saying, "Fuck me Peter's lived a life!" Next, he told us that he'd been a racing driver. He also said that he had the same Porsche that James Dean used to drive. He said that the axle was the very one from James's actual car. He told us that he was still doing this Porsche up.

We did think that he must have lived 20 lifetimes, but we liked him and we never took the piss out of him as he was an older fella. Anyway, me and Reidy are in Maldon walking down the High Street one day and we bump into him. Peter lived just outside of Maldon. He invites us back to his house for a cup of tea. We go there and I kid you not, on the wall were photographs of him on a motorbike surrounded by girls in skimpy clothing. Standing there with laurel wreaths around his neck at least four of five different pictures and you could see it was definitely him as a young man.

Below is a picture of him in a racing car, same thing more laurels around his neck. Next, he brings in his son's World Championship Kickboxing Belt. Now this is one thing I regret never buying. He had a ring that he'd made himself out of gold with a beautiful turquoise opal stone in it. It fitted me lovely. It was quite big but there was something very special about it. Unfortunately, I didn't have a lot of money in those days and so I didn't buy it. Now I wish I had. Everything this man had said to us in the gym was actually true. I would never have believed it and neither would Reidy. I remember Peter was slim and tanned and dressed a bit like a cowboy in cowboy boots and he had a moustache. About a month after that meeting at his home he dropped dead, and so we never saw him again. I always remember him as a very honest man.

Coming back to the present day, another great thing to happen to me is one of my daughters (I have three) Vicky managed to buy a house and has made a lovely job of extending it. She has a beautiful garden too and all her dogs with her and she's very happy with her husband Dave who is the love of her life.

My daughter Sarah is also in a lovely relationship and has three daughters of her own so I have three new granddaughters. Sarah is doing well, and she lives in Suffolk. My eldest daughter Marie, bless her heart, she's recently got married after a few relationship problems in the past. Thankfully through her work she's met a lovely, lovely fella called Trevor and so they got married. Now Marie has always been horse mad and had horses all her life.

She said to me, 'Dad I'm getting married, I've met a man and I liked and fell in love with him instantly.' Trevor 'Twinkle Toes' Wear as we call him because of his ballroom dancing. Anyway, Marie told me she'd like to get married where there were horses ideally, like on a farm perhaps, but she couldn't find anywhere.

Through James the artist, who painted the picture of me on the front cover of this book, [Chapter 10 tells more about meeting James and him subsequently painting Ronnie's portrait.] I met a lady called Vanessa Mitchell from The Cage in St Osyth. It's quite famous due to the witchcraft and witchfinder general connections. [A plaque on the building states the Cage was a medieval prison, and Ursula Kemp was imprisoned here before being hanged as a witch in 1582]. Anyway, it's supposedly a very haunted place and I went there to do a podcast with Michelle and Freddie [another medium and her sidekick.] Sometime later Vanessa got in touch with me and asked if I would do a show for her at the Brightlingsea Yacht Club.

In chapter 11 I describe in detail that meeting with Vanessa and Freddie at the much revered The Cage in St Osyth.

Now the Brightlingsea Yacht Club is a place I've never forgotten because I remember giving a message of a man coming through saying "Just like that!" I told the assembled crowd that day that everything about this man was Tommy Cooper. A lady put up her hand and she had a picture of him with his eulogy and he was wearing a Fez. I told her he was here doing Tommy Cooper impressions.

On that same night another lady called Jane said, "Would I be interested in doing a show for her?" I said to her "To be honest, not really as I tend to do my own shows if I can." But she persisted saying that it was a lovely big place that held a lot of people and that perhaps we could come to some sort of arrangement.

I asked what sort of place she owned, and she said it was a farm. I thought, "Wow!" How strange is that?" Now that's how spirits work. I said to Jane, "You haven't also got horses there, have you?" She confirmed she had, plus some alpacas. To cut a long story short I did a show for her and that cured the problem of a wedding venue for Marie and Trevor. Their wedding was absolutely amazing. Just a beautiful, beautiful wedding. So that's how spirit can intervene in our lives on this side sometimes.

It's a funny thing you might ask of Mediums working every day with spirits, you might say do we mourn? Of course we do!

Yes, we have the advantage of knowing that our loved ones are still around but it's still incredibly hard to give messages to your own family. For example, to give a message to my brother Paul it was hard because I already knew so much about him. When my dad passed, when I was 44 he would occasionally come through to me with a message for my mum. I remember once having to get her on the phone and ring her up because my dad [in spirit] insisted. I had to tell her that he'd said he knew about something yellow that she'd just put under the window.

It turned out that literally as I phoned her that day she'd been under the front window digging the flower beds in the garden and putting yellow daffodils in there.

There were a few other things that I told her that he told me and I couldn't have known so we can sometimes get messages for our own family. When you already know so much about a person it's hard. I have three daughters and as I've said I never read for them as I know too much about them. Also, maybe it's because I wouldn't like to hear [from spirit] what's likely to go on. My mum passed and I'm not going to say very much about her because to be honest I really didn't like the woman. She didn't really have a great deal of time for me when I was growing up. Once I was an adult I didn't have a great deal of time for her. So I never mourned her.

Michael, my brother I did mourn for, my niece Monique I did and Les I did, but not my mum. There's no spiritual law out there that says you've got to love someone because they're your family, there really isn't. If someone is a nasty piece of work and treats you badly then why should you love them? Just because they've got a title like Mum, Dad, Brother or Sister. So, no I'm not going to say too much more about my late mum. I never lost a minute's sleep or shed a tear for her when she passed. A couple of my brothers did, they had a very different relationship with her and that's also fine. It's ok they understood where I come from.

Even as a Medium you still miss the physical contact you have with your loved ones who have passed over. Les for example, my late father-in-law, lived next door so I was always seeing him. Me and Nicky had a breakup for a year and we got back together.

Pam, her mum, who I love dearly, she wasn't very keen on us getting back together. I think she tried to say to Nicky "Look you've had a couple of break ups, one for a few months and now one for a year, are you sure you're doing the right thing?" So understandably I was a bit nervous about coming back to see Nicky's parents again. I remember, I walked into the garden and there was Les. He quickly looked around to make sure no one was watching, and he came flying over to me, took my hand in both of his to shake it and said, "Good to have you back boy, good to have you back!"

We always had a great time together, so many barbecues and they have a very nice garden and at the very end is a shed with a bell on it. Out of his shed would always come the catapults, the bows and arrows, the air pistols and air rifles and whoever rang the bell got the drink in.

It was like always being in the company of a kid. Les truly was a lovely man and a great dad, very, very comical and always up to mischief.

As well as my own heartaches, as a medium, I have to relive other people's tragedies on a regular basis. This is a testimonial from Caroline who lives in Royston…

Picture caption: Neil and Daniel Wiltshire (Dan died suddenly on 29 March 2014).

The first time I saw Ronnie was at Elsenham Golf Club and I hadn't lived in the village for long. Ronnie got my fiancé, Pete, through who was killed in a car crash back in December 1980. He knew he was from London, but the accident happened up north and he knew I was a northerner (without having heard me speak). Ronnie also knew that I had been pregnant three times but only had one child and he also told me that Pete's baby, which I had sadly miscarried, was a boy and that the baby was with him.

Caroline with Pete

He also knew I had two brothers but that I was estranged from one and he told me that we would never be reunited (which we won't).

Another occasion I saw Ronnie was at a restaurant in Dunmow. This time I had persuaded my ex-partner, Neil (a sceptic) to accompany me. Almost immediately Ronnie asked who had lost a son and since nobody else had, he admitted he had (his son Dan died suddenly at the age of 39 in 2014). He told Neil that Dan was saying he was "The good dad" and Neil, who was absolutely gobsmacked, admitted to knowing what that meant. What he didn't tell Ronnie was that it was because Dan had been sexually abused by his stepfather as a child and it was Neil's evidence, given at the trial several years later when Dan was an adult, that put his stepfather away so he couldn't abuse any other children.

Ronnie also told Neil, "Dan is with someone riding a motorcycle." That was Neil's brother who also died at the age of 39, from leukemia. He also looked at me and said, "You're not his mum" and I said no, I wasn't. Then Dan must have been worried that he'd offended me because Ronnie said, "He's saying he hasn't got a problem with you, but you're not his mum." So, I laughed and said it was fine.

Shortly after that, Ronnie had my parents come through. My dad was killed in a crash in 1985 (first Pete, then him) and he had turned the car to the left, which put him between the coach and my mum.

My dad was killed in a crash in 1985

She didn't have a scratch, but he died almost instantly. I had always thought he turned instinctively but he told me he had done it to save my mum.

As we left the restaurant that night Neil turned to me and said, "How could he have known all that?"

Thanks and all the best,

Caroline Rogers

Celebrities have their own share of heartache, some of it we read about in the tabloids but sometimes they come to me for advice and guidance and validation that their loved ones are safely now on the other side of life.

I met Kate O'Mara there too

I've read for a few celebrities over the years. I went up to Manchester to meet some at the Reading Rooms. There were two actresses from the soap Coronation Street, and I met Kate O'Mara there too.

I was the only Medium who picked up the father of her son which she never disclosed to anyone. Her son sadly committed suicide. Her son was called Dickon, and I got the name of his father which no one had before. Everyone was sworn to secrecy about it.

She actually said to me at the time, "Ronnie you are the only one who has ever got that."

She was lovely, I remember when I was a kid around 17 or 18 I saw her on the telly and I thought, "Oh my God, you're beautiful!". So, to get to meet her, then become good friends and get to talk to her on the phone for ages as well as meeting her a couple of times too was incredible for me. Just before she passed, she got pneumonia, and she died in a hospice which is supported by fellow actors in the showbiz world. She was a tiny woman but very beautiful and very, very spiritual too.

Here's another celebrity, but also a good friend of mine Nicky Alan, a fellow Medium, who has written books about her experiences too .....

When you think of legends in the medium circuit, Ronnie is always the first medium that comes to people's minds. I adore that he has always stayed grounded and has never changed. I remember back in 2005 I was absolutely terrified as I was doing my first ever charity Evening of Mediumship in Benfleet, Essex in aid of SIDS (Sudden Infant Death Syndrome). I had been doing platform demonstrations in churches but had never faced the public out of the comfort of spiritualist centres. Despite Ron living on the other side of Essex he came all the way down to the venue and delivered some first class readings to a sellout crowd just to support me, and to help me feel that I wasn't alone. I have never forgotten that. Despite us now living far apart, if I needed to pick up the phone Ron would be there on the end wanting to help. He says it as it is. He is a superb ambassador for the Spirit World. He has brought comfort and proof of the afterlife to hundreds of thousands of people, and I am so proud to say, Ronnie Buckingham? Yep, I know him...

Love you Ron x

Nicky has been a freelance paranormal/spiritual writer since 2005

Her first book M.E Myself and I: Diary of a Psychic became an International Best Seller. Nicky's Second Book The Rise and Fall of Britain's Best Psychic Medium has become a No 1 International Best Seller also.

There is also an audible version available and has had multiple articles published. Nicky is the current columnist as the Psychic Detective in Take a Break's Fate and Fortune Magazine – UK and Australia. She investigates cold cases and mysteries using her psychic ability. Nicky has also appeared on TV shows such as Angels and worked alongside other internationally acclaimed Psychic's and Celebrities.

Nicky's third book Earthwalkers: Children of the Light is an amazing spiritual fiction book which is due out this year, and she has also created a new podcast show called SOULSPACE. The Podcast reached the Best Spiritual Show position in the UK in the second week of its launch. It is currently in the top 10% of most downloaded spiritual shows worldwide.

I also read for Tara Palmer-Tomkinson. In my first book I've included a picture of a drawing she did for me at the time.

On it she wrote, "To Ronnie, the man who knows me better than I do." Sadly, this lovely lady has also now passed over.

With Tara I predicted I could see her in a forest, and I told her at the time that it would lead to something which means you will be in a lot of adverts. She had an agent who told me afterwards, "You are too good Mr Buckingham." He said, "It wasn't a forest, it's a jungle." She was about to appear in *I'm a Celebrity Get Me Out of Here!* When she came out of the jungle, she was signed up by Walkers Crisps to do a load of adverts for them. She was lovely with a great pair of pins! We got on really well.

I was also at one point the Psychic Advisor to Big Brother and I did the Big Breakfast with Ian Laine too.

Atomic Kitten's Natasha Hamilton along with her mum

I've also read for the girls from Atomic Kitten, to name but a few. I talk more about other well-known names I've connected with further on in Chapter 10 of this book.

The true-life accounts included herein are each backed up with the original emails which I and my publisher still hold. Each person has very kindly given us their written permission to share their personal stories of readings with you.

As for the celebrity readings, as I don't have their permission, I wouldn't dream of sharing their personal details without it.

When I started the process of writing this second book, I appealed online for anyone wishing to share their stories to get in touch with me and to give their consent. I have only used those people who responded to that appeal. The many more, including those who are more well known to us, will always remain private, just between me and them – and the spirit world of course!

In the first book *Medium Rare*, I talk about little Jake Russell the kid who was run over and I'm now Godfather to his little brother who was born after him. I did a show and there was another medium there, a chap who was a French Canadian. He was also going to be on stage that night. He told me to go on first as I had a long drive back that evening. He was a nice man and quite local to the event which was being held in Bethnal Green. I went on stage and did my bit and he applauded me when I came off and we shook hands.

He said to me, "Oh I've got to tell you there was a little blonde-haired boy that stood beside you all throughout your part of the show, looking up at you. I think his name might be Jack?" Well, that was little Jake, I knew straight away.

The other medium told me that the little boy was looking up at me so lovingly as I stood there giving out messages.

I've had readings years and years ago when my own nan came through to the medium who was giving me a reading. As for me reading my own family, I can't because I already know too much about them. That's the kiss of death if you know too much about the person it doesn't work. I get emails from people, and I repeatedly tell them, don't tell me anything. When instead their email starts with, 'Oh I lost my mum to cancer can I have a reading?' I always tell 'em off. I say to them, "Don't tell me anything! That's my job to tell you. Just ask for a reading, that's all you need to say."

I can sense sometimes when my family are around me but I don't get that feeling that often. I already know that my own family who have passed are ok. So maybe that's why I can't read them because I don't need it. I don't need that reassurance so that's why it's not given to me.

One million percent I know that there is an afterlife, I know that. I've seen too much and done too much to know otherwise. I analyse myself. There were times when I first started out on this journey into mediumship, thinking is it just that I am a good guesser? Am I just mindreading? But each time the question was answered for me. Even when I do a reading for someone and part of the message they can't take. They very often text or email me back the following week saying, "Oh my goodness I've just remembered, or someone's told me, and I never knew it. So, you were right!"

I've also seen many spirits over the years, as plain as I see a normal living person, so I know it exists. I've got no fear of death itself. How I pass does worry me but not the actual going, that's a breeze, that's easy

CHAPTER 6

SIBLING BONDS

21 years ago, my friend Kate was going to have a medium come to her house for a meeting with some of her friends. I had lost my sister to cancer some months earlier and although I had been to spiritualist meetings she had never come through. I was a believer in spiritualism and mediums as both my gran and mother were very psychic.

I decided to go to Kate's for this meeting in the hope that I would get a reading. We were all sitting in Kate's front room waiting for the Medium. To be honest I was expecting a middle-aged woman, as at most meetings that is who the medium was. Saying that, I am sure there are lots of men who are just as good. Then who walks into the *room but this tall, blond, good looking, tattooed man - I was taken aback!*

Ronnie came to me first with a message from my sister. He gave me proof of my sister's death with her cancer and where it was. He also told me that my sister was wishing me and my husband a happy anniversary, which had just happened.

He said how it was our 33rd anniversary which it was. During the message he also said that they [the spirits] kept giving him the number 13 but he did not know why. A few months later my husband died on the 13th. I can only assume that is why he kept getting the number 13.

That message was so comforting from Ronnie. Thanks to him I had, at last, heard from my sister who I missed so much. Ronnie is such an amazing medium and wonderful person.

Mark Green

I've been seeing Ron for years for readings. I've attended group events, had dinner with Ron appearing as group setting after. I've also had a 1:1 booking with him. Each time I've been blown away by information he's given me. Firstly, he picked up on my brother's middle name of 'Praed' my brother Kieran unfortunately passed away at 22 months old after falling in our family pond. Ron was able to tell us that Kieran was going to look at a Moorhen he had spotted on the water, at the time.

Kieran Joshua Praed Reynolds who passed away aged just 22 months

He also described his outfit he was wearing that day, the family dog that was with him at the time and has since passed over and is with him now.

Another time I went to see Ron at Bensons Bar in Braintree and my grandad, who was a prison officer, came through. Ron mentioned my grandad was in uniform and 'liked a drink' the only other thing I was told that time was that I was pregnant, and it was a boy. Five weeks later I found out I was pregnant!

Eight months later along arrived Thomas Albert Praed – I gave him the same middle name as my late brother Kieran.

Lastly, I'd like to tell you about the 1:1 I had with Ronnie. This wasn't booked in my name I bought it as a gift but decided I wanted the appointment myself. Along I went and Ron looked shocked when he opened the door to see that it was me. On this occasion I had to put the recording we did that day in the bin as Ron mentioned something that I'd never told a soul – literally no one!!! I was totally wiped away by what he said as soon as I sat down. Ron just came out with this information I'd never spoke of.

He also mentioned I've lots of children around me to which I replied, "I've three children but my partner has his own as well?"

Reece and Emma with twins Ronnie and Roman

Then Ron said, "Twins. I'm seeing twins here." My partner at the time was a twin so I assumed that's what he meant. I was nodding away listening to his every word when Ron said,

"The guy you're going to settle down with forever Emma you know him already." I thought yup that's my current boyfriend. I assumed and also he's the twin. Ron continued, "It's a voice you like…South London - deep voice." That was also true as I'm a sucker for a good voice.

That relationship ended soon after my reading with Ronnie. Randomly I bumped into an old school friend who has the perfect voice and a lovely accent. His dad's family are from the East end of London. I am happy to report that we now have our twin boys Ronnie and Roman plus my other original three children. Ronnie really is gifted; he knows more about my life and me than I do myself.

Emma

CHAPTER 7

SPIRIT CHILDREN

We attended an evening with Ronnie Buckingham at Marconatos in Hoddesdon. We had been to see him before and was amazed at how good he was. We attended another evening with some friends, one of whom was hoping to get a message from his mum, but it turned out it was our turn.

Ronnie said he had a little boy who had been stillborn and was giving him the letter A. I was nervous but excited as this was the first time since having Albie seven years ago that anyone had got him. So, I nervously raised my hand and Ronnie continued. He said that he was around 2-3 days late which was spot on and he also said he was around 8lb 12 again that was spot on. Ronnie told us that he was waving a Star of David and at this point my husband said that his grandad was Jewish and he had messaged my husband literally that day!

Ronnie described Albie's grave and his actual plot which was also spot on. He knew that we visited his grave most weekends too. He told us that Albie was around us all the time and gave us signs and also that he was a cheeky little boy!

This reading was everything to us as Ronnie was the first medium to give us our little boy.

Thank you Ronnie and we will be back x

Sophie Hendy

It all started when my friend Jacqui called on the 12th of January 2019. She rang to tell me, "Deb I have booked tickets to see Ronnie. Do you want to come? It's on the 19th of February in Harold Wood?"

I said yes straight away as I had always heard fantastic things about Ronnie.

We took our places, Jacqui had got us excellent seats. I was quite excited as it was my first time seeing him. As the evening began, I remember thinking that he was as great as I'd heard. Ronnie had already given three readings before he got to me.

He had turned to my direction and my nerves kicked in as I just knew I was next.

Ronnie said, "Can someone take a son here who had an impact collision?" My friend quickly put her hand up saying, "Yes!" pointing at me saying I had lost my son.

Ronnie said he was a young man maybe 20, I replied 28. He said, "Oh he looks younger. Then he asked if he was around 5ft 7ins tall and I replied yes. He told me what a good-looking guy he was and he laughed saying, "A bit of a ladies man!" Ronnie went on to describe his love for the gym and lifting weights too.

He asked if he had passed on a motorcycle? I replied yes and he told me he passed straight away and that it was quick (a great comfort as ambulance workers had said he was alive and in pain for an hour.)

Ronnie told me that he passed near home, which was true and that he passed on a Thursday around 5.30pm. I remember thinking, how on earth would you know any of this?

He asked if I was with his father, I replied, "Hell No!" and everyone laughed. Ronnie asked who Mark was and I said, "That's his father." He asked me if owned a pub. I was puzzled and said no then he replied, "Oh does he's father have a drink problem?" I said yes, he's an alcoholic then Ronnie also told me there was violence in the relationship which was true.

He continued by saying that's why my son and his father didn't have a good relationship, he's telling me that his father was a wife beater.

Ronnie stumped me when he next asked me, "Your son had a love for football? I replied back saying no he didn't. He insisted saying, "He does, he's holding a football." I said again no he doesn't and to be honest I felt myself getting angry at this point as I knew it was untrue. Undeterred Ronnie said that he knew he was right about what he was telling me. He said, "Ok then but can you explain why he's holding a football with CHELSEA written on it?"

I just gasped, that was it! Chelsea is his sister, my eldest daughter's name. She is just two years younger than my son Simon. At that moment the room went quiet and completely still with everyone so shocked by what they had just witnessed.

Debbie Pusey

We went to see Ronnie on a night out at Wick Lodge Bar & Restaurant in Jaywick Lane, Clacton-on-Sea. There were three of us, myself, my husband Les, and our friend Debbie. It was the second time we had seen Ronnie there, but the first time for my friend Debbs. She was both nervous and excited at the same time, as she had been to see a few mediums and her son and hubby had never come through to her. Well, this night was to be different for her, very, very different!

This is Ronnie, Bebb's son

As the evening wore on, I remember we had an interval, after the interval, Ronnie said he had a young man that had come through to him, who had died in a road accident.

For some strange reason I just knew it was Debb's son who was also called Ronnie.

I immediately elbowed her, so she paid special attention. I still at this point don't think it had sunk in, but I remember I had tears in my eyes, so I listened to what Ronnie had to say. I knew her son had died in an accident along Clacton seafront. Her son Ronnie told the medium Ronnie that he was ok, among other things and that he was with Dad. Ronnie [the medium] then ended the reading, but as he was about to walk off the stage he turned round and shouted out, "Oi Wheeler!"

Instantly I knew that message was also for Debbs my friend. As it was her husband and it even sounded like him, if that's even possible? It was amazing. I looked at my friend with tears in my eyes (again!) and we both knew it was her Mick, no one ever called Debbs "Wheeler" apart from her hubby Mick!!

Mick her hubby

That same night my hubby's brother also came through to him. He had only been gone one year and sadly died from cancer very quickly with no time for goodbyes. Instantly we knew it was Les's brother Colin. Ronnie was able to tell us Les's birthday. He said, "What does the 15th of December mean to you?" Les was stunned, so I said to Les, "It's your birthday."

I think at this point Les was still too stunned for it to register fully. Ronnie also said he saw bars on a window with a face behind them, we laughed at that as my Les had spent a short spell in prison in his youth!

Although none of my loved ones have come through to me yet at any of Ronnie's night readings it's ok, because I know the afterlife exists. I've had personal experiences that prove there is an afterlife. I'm just happy to sit, watch and listen to other people's experiences. It's always so emotional!! In our own personal experience, what Ronnie can do is amazing. He brings great comfort to many people.

Much love

Suzette Bakker

I've seen Ronnie on numerous occasions, but a memorable one was when we went to the Stevenage Football Hall. My daughter had sadly lost her little girl at full term, 39 weeks and 3 days. Ronnie looked directly at us and actually said, "I really don't like these, but I've a baby here who has passed."

It was my Harriet who the baby had come to be near. Ronnie told Harriet about her losing Elsie-May, and that there was nothing she could have done, it wasn't her fault. He went on to say Elsie-May's birth weight which was absolutely correct at 4lb 1 oz.

Elsie May born on the 16th September

That Mummy and Daddy had separated, that Daddy was then a prison officer (and made a joke about that) and that there was a little sister born called Darcie. Ronnie also told Harriet she'd got a tattoo and where it was on her body. He told Harriet how many pictures she'd got up in her house of Elsie-May which was correct and also mentioned her birthday day being in September and the 16th.

Ronnie was amazing. Now we regularly come and see him and our gorgeous 'little angel' often pops in to say hello via Ronnie. We can't thank him enough for the comfort and upliftment he has brought to us and so many others. Kind regards and love

Angi Bentley and Harriet Wilson

Adam - He wants you to know he's alright

I went to Ronnie in Rosedale sports club in Cheshunt on 7/7/23 Me and my mum and my mate Sharon. There wasn't many seats as we got there late so we ended up right up on the front row. Ronnie comes over to us all and starts his reading he says, "I feel someone around you." Ronnie told me about my cousin passing over including what dog he had.

Aunty Anne

Saying "Paul is still here I guarantee you that, he says he had a tattoo and tattoos in memory of him." He also said he had a dog, it was a little thing, I want to say a Staffordshire bull terrier." Ronnie carried on, "It was very quick, they hit him on a Friday. He is one of four kids.

He wants you to know he is alright." He also said he was cockney. Ronnie also told me of my baby boy in heaven. He said, "I hope I'm wrong here, but did you lose a baby?" I said, "No but I did have a termination." Ronnie explained in the spirit world it's the same kinda thing, saying, "I would say he was a boy." He also went on to tell me about my auntie Anne who passed in January. I was amazed and feel so much better to know they are all ok. For me Ronnie was by far the best I've seen, thanks so much.

Sinead from Enfield x

I and my husband Stuart had the pleasure of a private reading with Ronnie in January 2024. My Father-in-law but, most importantly, our son Lewis came through.

Lewis the night before he passed

He was spot on with nearly everything. There were, and still are, a few names that we cannot get to the bottom of, but my husband has a massive family.

Ronnie said that Lewis was a good-looking lad with lots of hair but not long, which it was. He described what Lewis was wearing when we laid him to rest and what was in the coffin with him (a roll up that a mate had put in his pocket and a bottle of Jack Daniels.) Ronnie said that Lewis said thank you for these. He knew we had kept some hair and that we have had a tattoo in his memory.

He continued saying that he didn't take his own life which to us was comforting. Ronnie also knew he drowned and that it was a gravel pit or something like that. It was a reservoir.

He described to us a big dog like an Alsatian with him (my dad had an Alsatian). He said that Lewis sees the animals buried in the garden (a budgie and two ferrets). Ronnie also mentioned coconuts or, to be precise, two halves which made us chuckle as knowing our son he could have worn them at some point in his life. But then we realised we have the old coconut shells still hanging in the garden from feeding the birds. One of the things that spooked us a bit was that Ronnie mentioned someone close has a brain tumour. That in fact is my husband, he was wearing a hat that day and there was no way of him knowing.

I have also been to three separate group readings and Lewis came through every time. Everything Ronnie said was on point. We really appreciate the reading and comfort he has given us.

I still have the recording from our private reading.

Thank you from the bottom of my heart

Tracy Saggers

My name is Carol Walker. I have been seeing Ronnie Buckingham at his shows for the last two years since my son passed away. The first time I went along was around eight weeks after my son passed and I was anxious that I wouldn't hear from my beloved son as it might have been too soon. The day I went along the room was full of people.

Carol's beloved son Lee

The first thing Ronnie said was, "I have a young man here, late twenties." My son was 40 years old when he passed but looked very young for his age.

Ronnie said he died on a Monday, which was the day he was found. Ronnie said he died of an overdose of drugs and that he didn't commit suicide. He then said to me, "Why is there a question mark over his death?" I said that the police are investigating as there were two guys that had passed in the same area. Ronnie went on to say that he was a London boy, north London, Edmonton, which was also correct that's where my son was born. He said he was found in a flat on the second floor. My son moved into a flat which was on the second floor, above shops, five days before passing.

I'm ok now mum, I'm ok

Ronnie told me that my son passed quick. He said that he fell to sleep which was the best comfort for me.

He also told me that my son was troubled which was correct but that he is saying, "I'm ok now mum I'm ok."

He was laid to rest in a Spurs top

My son had also said that I gave him a great sendoff. Ronnie said to me, "Why am I seeing football?" My son loved Spurs and so he was laid to rest in a Spurs top and had a Spurs flag on his coffin. All the funeral flowers being blue and white.

Ronnie went on to tell me, "He is telling me you split the ashes."

At the time, people were saying I should give my dad some ashes but I refused. Then I clocked it, I had Lee around my neck, made from some of his ashes into glass.

You gave him a great send off

He also said my son had two boys and there had been a dispute about him seeing his boys. This was also correct and had been going on for around seven years.

Ronnie also mentioned some names which were all correct and that I have a tattoo that's my son's name.

I now always go to the Braintree meetings and my son comes through every time. For those who are sceptical and think that Ronnie would recognise me, you are wrong. The last time I went, there must of been over two hundred people in there. I'm a true believer in the afterlife.

Regards Carol

Milly, who is Charlie's furry sister

I was in the audience of one of Ronnie's shows in his hometown of Braintree about six years ago.

He told the audience that had a message from a young girl about 17yrs old who wouldn't stop talking and I remember Ronnie laughed. I'm not sure but I think he said something along the lines of she wasn't alive on this side and at that point my ears pricked up. I sat there and wondered if this was my daughter Lauren who I had sadly lost through a stillbirth pregnancy. Ronnie went on to mention a jewellery box with music (yes a ballerina jewellery box) I then said I can relate to this and Ronnie proceeded with the message he told me "You kept her scan pictures in there ". He then went on to say that Lauren thinks my dog is adorable and scatty. Ronnie said my dog's name Molly initially and I said no then he said Millie which is correct.

He went on to say that Molly is my son Charlie's furry sister as he is my only living child as I'm unable to have more children.

Ronnie also mentioned a flower, saying that Lauren liked it . When she was born and taken away from me in the hospital, I gave the midwife a single flower to put with her whilst she was cremated by the hospital. Everything Ronnie said was spot on. I was so at ease with myself after that night knowing that Lauren is looking down on me and my family.

Keep doing what you do best Ronnie xx

CHAPTER 8

FIGHTING FIT

In the past I've also been a gym instructor and I've always trained, all of my life. In fact, back in 2020 when I was 66, I did the London to Brighton Cycle Ride. I took part and raised just over £5k for the British Heart Foundation through my Facebook friends

The organisers, London Marathon Events (LME) told me for a 17 stone man of my age, if I could do it in around seven hours, that would be a good result. I actually came in at four hours and 17 minutes. I was also proud to make it to the very top of Ditchling Beacon [Brighton]. That's something which I always swore I would do.

The lads I know at the bike shop, where I go to get the bikes tuned, they'd all tried it. All four of them, even on the tandem and they never made it to the top. The ones riding on the tandem collapsed before they got to the top just because it's so steep. However, my mindset is if I set my mind on achieving something I will do it. So, I did make it to the top with a witness.

However shortly afterwards, once I got home, I kept feeling faint. I'd stand up and almost fall down again and have to sit down. The wife managed to get me into the Doctors surgery where she worked at the time. They diagnosed me with both an Atrial Flutter and AF (Atrial Fibrillation) and Polycythemia vera (PV). So, I was away having blood drained and had to be put on blood thinners. Sadly, that has ended my cycling days. My wife still swears that the problem I now have with my heart is because I wouldn't give up and I wouldn't get off my bike like everyone else does on that incredibly steep incline towards the summit. For me, because I said I would do it, I had to keep going. I'm a typical Capricorn, it just had to be done. Nicky says I'm my own worst enemy in many ways.

Me with what looks like a blue flower on my nose!

I thought I'd talk a little bit about how sometimes you can give messages in the most bizarre situations.

One was when I was going into theatre at my local hospital to have skin cancer cut away from my nose.

Several of the nurses recognised me and said, 'Oh god we've got a bit of a celebrity in here today!' So, the doctor who was Indian asked what it was I did. The nurses told him I was a medium.

He was putting the injections into my nose before they started to cut out the cancer cells. No word of a lie the Indian doctor's dad came through, there and then!

So, I was actually able to give the doctor a message in the theatre. I didn't mean to, but I had the doctor in tears! The reading came through in great detail. I remember telling him that his dad passed very young, maybe only around about his 30s with a heart attack, which he confirmed was correct. I remember saying to the Doctor, "You've only got one brother there's only two of you." Which is odd as Indian families are often quite large. Because his dad passed young, he'd only had two sons. I was able to tell him, "You dad is telling me that you have one son and one daughter that he never knew. He's telling me he has seen them spiritually. I also told him that his brother only had one son. I went on to say, "I know what you do obviously, you're a plastic surgeon. As for your brother, your dad is showing me that your brother is surrounded by money. The doctor told me what I had said was indeed correct and that his brother was big in the banking world and was a very, very wealthy man.

Recently I had to have my knee redone, a patella resurfacing (partial knee resurfacing). Directly I came round in the recovery room at the hospital, I was giving messages out to the nursing staff who work in recovery.

Also, whilst I was in the ward, I was there for two or three days recovering, as I had a slight complication due to being on blood thinners, I gave out at least another half a dozen messages to the nurses there too. So, let's just say I'm now very popular in Broomfield and Springfield Hospital.

A lot of people say to me, "How do you relax and turn off? Every day since I became a medium, I'm dealing with death and other people's grief. For me it's the gym.

Left: Graham (aka the German, Shakespeare Wordsworth and Arthur-writus), George, Me, Gary and Emma (front)

The gym for me is my lifeline. It's where I get grounded again. I still go regularly, although less so lately due to having my knee done. There are a few of us all between the ages of 60 through to 78. George Jenkins is one of them. He's an old power lifter, originally from the Bethnal Green Weightlifting club. George is a lovely, lovely fella. He's one of these people who likes to be given a bit of stick and believe me he also gives plenty out! One of the other guys I train with at the gym is Gary Parmenter.

Gary has been in a few body building shows in his time. (He's won fuck all!)

However, he's a lovely fella too and very knowledgeable. Nowadays he does tyres. If you've rimmed your tyres or ruined your wheels he'll do it for you. Smashin' fella. Last, but not least, there's Graham Jarvis. Graham is an ex-marine, so he's seen some action. He's also the youngest of us all at the gym who train together regularly.

Over the time we've known each other and trained together, George has come up with a series of nicknames for us all. Way back when I first met him, he was telling us that Graham had someone who was of German heritage in his family so Graham became known as *The German*. Graham is one of these people that when he trains, he tends to get a pad and pen and writes down all of the reps he did and the weights he's lifted. So, George notices this and now Graham has now become known as either *Shakespeare* or *Wordsworth*. More recently Graham has been complaining about his arthritis. George has now started calling Graham, *Arthur-writus! (Arthur for short)*.

So, it does change from time to time. From the minute I go in there, and I've trained at CHF for 14 years, it's piss-taking from the moment I arrive. It's all done in good humour though as we all of us give it and we all take it too. Then there's little Emma Corrigan at the gym too working out and she doesn't get the stick we get but she's a great kid. Emma always sticks up for the one person that day who is getting the most stick from the rest of us.

Might be me one day when they are pulling my leg about how fat I am. Or it might be George because we all give him plenty of stick.

Years ago, George had had a terrible accident. He was run over by a forklift truck. Subsequently they said he would never walk again. He's proved that wrong. At 78 and still down the gym he puts his crutches to one side and still trains really, really hard alongside us. A lovely, lovely man. George actually said to me that without the gym he wouldn't want to be here anymore. He gets there about seven in the morning, and he stays there afterwards and has a coffee 'til about 11am. Whereas I get there about eight and I'm gone by about half nine in the morning. I don't do the coffee thing. They are all great fellas, and that is my relief from the many, many readings I do.

I go in there and train and enjoy all of the great banter between us all. They are all good lads and it really is funny when we all get together. The one thing that Emma did agree with me about was, one day when it was George's turn to have some stick, that when he gets halfway through an exercise, he puffs his cheeks out. Now I said, "Don't he look like Popeye?" That's the only time I've even known Emma to agree with me, she said, "Do you know what Ronnie, I can't argue with that." Hence George is now known to us all as *Popeye or sometimes Wobbly Man* because he falls over a lot, but bless him, he always gets back up.

The gym is what keeps me sane.

The gym is what keeps me sane. When you're dealing with death and misery every day you need some form of escapism.

I wouldn't say I'm everyone's cup of tea but, 98% of people who I've read for, have been happy with their reading and have either come back again or recommended me.

With my first book *Medium Rare*, it's a book that men read. Their wives bought the book initially and then said to their husbands he's been an armed robber; he's been in prison and then was a bouncer! So, the amount of women who have told me, "My husband couldn't put your book down." I'm quite rough and ready and not what you might expect from a male medium.

I remember I did a show once and a man in the audience who was being a bit of an arse (you always get one!). I asked are there any questions and he put his hand up and said, "Why are most male mediums gay?" so quick as a flash I said, "Give us a kiss, and I'll tell you!" He went 20 shades of red and everyone laughed.

It's quite strange but whatever the spirit world throws at me, I always seem to bounce back. I mean I've had cancer of the nose, all sorts of things. I worked with Mike Rollands the famous psychic pianist once. Steve Barry who was a trance medium and I, we did a show together years ago. I'd had a terrible time, I'd nearly died after coming out of Broomfield Hospital after an operation that went wrong. I was literally in a wheelchair. My haemoglobin levels were very, very low and this show I was supposed to do was for charity and it was sold out.

On the night, the other two mediums did their thing but on that particular night, I was the main attraction.

So, I was pushed on stage in a wheelchair with a blanket over my knees. I still had a catheter bag on the side. The spirit world said to me, 'Six messages, just six messages." There were some very old school mediums there that night also. One of which was Eileen Roberts who was stricter than strict. She was President of the British Association of Mediums or something like that. She sat in the audience that night. Now she terrified mediums because she was old school and would tear mediums to bits.

Understandably, I wasn't my normal swearing, jokey self. I just sat in my wheelchair on the stage and gave out these six messages. Eileen came up to me afterwards on stage, she took my hand and told me they were some of the best messages she'd ever heard. I remember I was so proud of that. However, I felt physically terrible, but you get there and the spirit world just take over.

I've been to shows in the past when I've felt sick and bilious and once I start working it all just disappears. It's like going into a totally different zone. You forget everything. So, whether it's bandages on your nose, limping using sticks, whatever is wrong with you it all just disappears. It's like with Bella my beloved pet dog I talked about in Chapter 4, I knew she was in a terrible way, and I was worried about her but it all got taken away 'til after the show. So that's just an insight into how the spirit world lets you work. The thing is people need these messages to come through. People need to know that their loved ones are ok. I consider myself to be very lucky to have been given the gift and I'm very lucky to be able to do what I can.

A word now about my tattoos. I'm well known as the Tattooed Medium. My dad hated tattoos and when I still

My dad hated tattoos

lived at home, I very much admired this Scottish Boxer called Jimmy Stanley. He also had lots of tattoos and because I'd built a bit of muscle by then I thought they looked really cool.

In those days the nearest Tattoo artist to me was a terrible tattooist. It was a fella called Vic Shipton and you'd go in there and it was very dirty. He'd have prostitutes having dots put on them and he was always on the drink. At the time it was the only tattooist I could get to. They became rather addictive, but they were terrible, terrible tattoos. I remember here [Ronnie shows me his right forearm] where the dragon is now it used to be a fish. It was meant to be a shark, it looked more like a sardine! Above it was a little bird which looked like it had flown into a wall! It had Mum & Dad written on it. On my chest I had St George but without the dragon and it also looked truly terrible. Just all shocking tattoos. I'll never forget I didn't tell my Dad that I had tattoos or else he'd have gone mental. I always wore clothes around him to cover them up.

So, where we lived together in the pub at the time, I was about 16 coming on 17 and I'd had all of these tattoos done. This particular day I had a date with someone. You know what it's like. My bedroom in that house was really close to the bathroom. So, I jumped into the bathroom and showered ready for my date.

I put a towel around my waist to nip back into my bedroom and as I opened the door, my dad was standing outside the bathroom door, waiting to go in the bathroom himself!

He saw my body covered in tattoos and he literally staggered backwards, and he called my mum. He called, "Ethel! Come and look at this silly bastard. He looks like a roll of wallpaper!" He was actually a very funny man my dad, he was a comedian. He was very, very witty. I remember my mum had been a very good, professional singer but my dad wasn't the sort of man who liked to socialise. He didn't like going out for meals and meeting friends, but he was very funny.

When they had the pub they had a barn dance one night. What you had to do that evening was perform something off the telly like an advert. I remember some of the nutcases in the pub. Crissy Brace, God bless his heart, he arrived dressed in a nappy – as a Johnson's Baby. Everyone that night was doing all of these different adverts. My mum said to my dad, "Look it's your night, you're the publican, you've got to do something too." Dad told her he was ready to go just as he was that night.

For the night to make it authentic, they'd made like a pretend giant television. The idea was each person would walk behind the 'TV Screen' and do their advert. So, my mum says, "Where's your outfit?" My dad was insistent he had it covered and everything was ok. When it comes to my dad's turn, he crept down behind the TV screen, keeping really low, and everyone said what fucking advert is that Ronnie? My dad told them, "Head n Shoulders!"

That's how he was. This Chris Brace was a big drinker and a watch repairer and he was a lovely man. He had to go into hospital one time to have a heart operation and he disappeared from his hospital bed. They found him in a pub in London, at the bar, with his arse hanging out of his hospital gown, having a drink! He was the nicest man.

My mum had these lovely flower boxes outside the pub and Chris brought her some seeds saying, I brought these for you some beautiful flowers. When they grew, they were actually carrots and onions! When they came through, my mum went mental!! That's the sort of pub that it was, I remember we had pram races there too.

Anyway, back to my tattoos. I had them done and as I've said they were really terrible ones. As time went on, they weren't like the inks you get now. They lost all of their shape as the ink began the run and so you couldn't really see what they were. They started to look just like bits of colour. So, when I reached the age of 66 and 67 I had new ones put over the whole lot.

They all mean something to me. The one on my left arm is Merlin the soothsayer physic, which refers to me. Underneath in French, coz we lived in France it says, *'You look but I really see, you listen but I really hear.'* I've also always liked crows. I don't know why, so I had the Druid done as they were very much into that sort of thing too, Mediumship and Mother Earth and I'm into that a bit too. I also had a little Robin added there as well, as an extra. So together they covered all of the previous older tattoos.

I had the Robin as they are sent as spirit messengers. You find whenever someone is bereaved, you'll always find Robins turn up in the garden. They say that the Robin had the red breast because originally it was like a sparrow but that it was at the foot of the cross when they crucified Jesus. They say that the blood from Jesus dropped onto the plain bird's breast and nowadays that's why you see a Robin red breast.

This tattoo on my right arm is a mystical dragon with a crystal ball. I had that because dragons are quite a symbol when it comes to Mediumship due to their spiritual nature. This tattoo also on my arm is in the memory of my late father-in-law Les Jones who I mentioned in Chapter 5. That's exactly the tattoo that Les used to have but his was on his hand. It's like a blue bird and all of the brothers and his daughter had the same one. It just says *In Memory of the Legend Les Jones*. This symbol here is because I'm also a Capricorn. On my forearm is a black and red heart with horns at the top to show that there is good and bad in everyone. Just to say that everyone has a darker side to them. This tattoo also on the same arm is when I married Nicky. We'd been together 15 years by then, but we married on that date. So I'd been married before and Nicky had been widowed so it was two hearts joined together and there's also a clock showing the time we got married with a cupid too. Finally, there's a third eye, which stands for clairvoyance. Oh, and also a charm symbol because I have a love of anything to do with the Vikings. This one here, we once stayed in a hotel in Bournemouth, and it was where Edward had had meetings there years ago with Wallace Simpson.

Evidentially at the time one of the Royal Press Agents went to King Edward VIII at that time and said, "There's a lot being said about you and her and it's not looking good." His response was for me the politest way in the world of saying my favourite word – Bollocks! He said "They Say! What Say They? Let Them Say." I think he was saying I don't give a Fuck" and that's my philosophy too. So, all of my tattoos have a story behind them now.

The one on my chest is now also redone. He added a dragon so St George is on his horse with now a dragon and that's because I'm very patriotic. I've also got some others, but I don't show them off to anyone but Nicky!

In my first book I opened up about my criminal past and there were a couple of stories that I left out. I've included them in this my second book firstly to make you laugh. Also to show that despite being a wrong un all those years ago, the saying *Honour Among Thieves* is something I lived by and still truly believe in.

I was always honourable with anyone I worked with, and they were honourable with me. However, occasionally you worked with people you don't really know, and they turn out to be wrong uns. On this one particular occasion it was a three-way thing. There was a chap who knew of a shop/come warehouse which had lots of expensive clocks inside. This chap knew of a buyer for all of these clocks if someone would steal them. There was another chap that I knew, he wasn't a great mate, but I knew him. You couldn't have called us friends I just knew him around.

This fella who tipped us off about the clocks told me and him all about where they were and that he wanted them stolen. So, I said to this chap, the one I knew of but wasn't a friend, "What's my gain is your gain. So do you fancy it?" He said, "Yeah, why not."

So, we went and looked the place over and I thought to myself, "Yes we can do this." There were some lovely clocks inside, pretty carriage clocks and just basically all sorts of different kinds of clocks.

In those days we used to research what were the best ones to take. From that research I could tell that there were a lot worth taking. Anyway, the chap who was setting it up got in touch with me a week later. He said he'd been approached by the other bloke (the one I'd decided to do the job with) who had told him to expect these clocks within a week. Which was odd because I'd already told this chap that we would do the deed in three weeks' time together.

At that point the penny dropped. I thought, "He's rode me out and put someone else on it." When we'd gone to check the job out, I was the one who suggested how we'd do it and how we'd get in etc. because that was my game.

Anyway, my normal working partner was away for a few weeks so I couldn't ask him, but I was livid. Because I'd gone along with him and been very honest and said this is what we'll do, steal them and then split the money. I thought to myself, "Fuck it! I ain't having this!"

We had a van and an estate car at the time, not in our name, but parked up all over in places that we used. I knew my mate who was away wouldn't mind, so I took our van. I went along and I did the job myself, on my own. Yes, it was a big, big risk but I was young then and fuming. It took me several journeys, but I took these clocks. I filled this motor up, late at night. Driving home I didn't think that the owner would keep these clocks all wound up, but he did. I think it was about 11 or maybe midnight because all of a sudden, my van sounded like a Tony Bell Ice Cream van! These clocks in the back of the van were all chiming at once! The noise was unbelievable!!

I'm driving along in the dark, by myself, killing myself laughing. I took them to what we call a 'flop' basically a place where we hid things. Of course, the next day the chap who was going to steal them with me was on the phone to me saying, "They've all been stolen overnight!!" I was able to tell him, "It's ok it's me mate." but I told him, "You're getting nothing. I know what you had planned to do. You were going to fuck me over on this job." I told him "You want to make something of it? We'll have a meet up and if you want to go to war over it, that's what we'll do." I did manage to get rid of the clocks, even though they continued to chime, but I've never forgotten that.

I'd never turn anyone over, and I'd be very hurt if anyone ever thought that I did. Now also years ago, there was a fella who was local to me and did a little bit of door work. He was German.

I did a couple of bits of work with him, but he was a bit bottley for my liking. He was very nervous around any work we did. Always saying to me, "Come on, come on, let's go!" When we were on a job together. I did put a few quid his way. I remember I nicked a safe with him one night. I knew where it was, he wanted to go but I picked it up and carried it out. I was the one who broke it open, and he got half the money. So, he was ok. Anyway, I was due to go and see him this one day and I drove over to his house, which was on the outskirts of Colchester sort of way. When I got there, there was no one in. So, I got back in my car which was a Jaguar at the time, and I went home again. About an hour or maybe an hour and a half later he turns up with his screechy-voiced brother saying, "Did you go to our house?" Of course, I said "Yeah, I did, why what's the matter?"

Now let's wind the clock back to a couple of weeks before. I'd been in their house and this brother had hid all this gold he had. Sovereign rings and some other bits in a drawer. Now I swear to God, I would never, ever steal off my own type of people. At the time I didn't even register it.

So, going back to this particular day. He knows I've been over to their house which I declared I had in all innocence. It turns out his gold was gone. He's come straight round to accuse me. I said to this brother, "Don't be fucking daft, that ain't my game, why would I do that?"

In the past the German guy and I had a few play fights and I'd always ended up putting him on his arse. He was very wary of me.

He also knew that his brother couldn't fight his way out of a paper bag. The pair of them on this day started to aggravate me I told them to search my car, which they actually did, which annoyed me. I said, "Go in have a search around my house." Which they also did and of course they found nothing. To this day he still thinks it was me. That really pissed me off.

Anyway, a girl I used to see; he went on to see later on. I got on very well with her. He in fact married her in the end but it didn't last. I told her it wasn't me and she told me, "He still thinks it was you and he tells everyone it was you." I told her that I knew that, but I said, "He wouldn't admit that to me!"

Some years later I ended up in Norwich prison with a fella I knew whose name I won't give. He was also much, much better, long-term mates with this particular German character and like me he also hated his brother. He said to me, "The brother reckons you stole his gold." Again, as before, I told him I hadn't. Then he laughed and said, "No I know you didn't, because I did!" He went on to tell me that he was a great mate but that he couldn't stand his brother. "He said, the weird thing is his brother had lent me his motorbike. I went there to return it, but they weren't in. So instead, I went inside, stole his gold and shot off again on his motorbike!" Obviously, the neighbour hadn't seen him that day, only me.

At the time he begged me not to tell this fella what he'd said. There's been many occasions since when I've wanted to, but I never have.

There are not many occasions when something said about me has hurt but that did hurt and I felt really put out by that, being accused of something that I hadn't done.

Even now I can't stand grasses. Don't get me wrong, if I see someone robbing a bank, I'd step out of their way and say good luck to you boys, as long as they don't hurt anyone. Saying that I would step in if someone was being mugged or raped. I don't believe in stealing off your own or hurting people. Even back in the days when we went to work, if we did robberies, no one got hurt. I didn't believe in hurting people. To be honest most people will give you the things if you threaten them, without having to touch them. Some people are just bullies.

Another funny story involves some of the people I worked the doors with. In those days they knew that I was also a ducker and a diver. One day I got a phone call to say there was a lorry load of wine for sale. They wanted six grand for it, which was a lot of money then, I'm going back to the late 1980's.

By this time, my prison days were well and truly over but this sounded too good to be true. So, I've gone over to the Southend area. I had a meet with these lads, and they've got this lorry hidden up, full of wine. The girl I happened to be with at the time really understood wine. So, she told me which were ok, not so good and those which were very good indeed. I had to drop the bombshell to these lads I said to them, "Look I haven't got the money. I haven't got six grand round me to buy it."

They said that they really needed to get rid of it as it's sort of hot. Saying, "We need to get rid of it all."

At the time I had a new Ford Orion Ghia. It was all paid for and done. That's what I'd spent my money on. I said, "I'll swap you my car for the wine." I knew that the car would sell easily, they'd get five and a half or six grand easily for it. So, they agreed and said to me, "But if you get caught, taking the wine away, then the car is still ours." I agreed as a deal is a deal. I gave them my car and I went and borrowed a big, transit Luton off someone and went back to get this wine. I took the expensive ones and the mid ones and a few of the cheapies but I couldn't take it all as there was a lot there.

I remember I had to pump the van tires with way more air than they should have had in them because it was on the axles. Bringing it all home, going up hills I was driving at about 10mph. How I never got nicked over that I'll never know. Someone up there must love me!

I got it back to where I was staying with this particular girl. She had an out of the way place. Over the next two days I made myself busy. Working in clubs and knowing people who worked in restaurants, I made loads of journeys in her car. Just non-stop, running here and there and I sold the lot. I made quite a bit of money and so I went and bought myself another nice car. This time it was a Peugeot 309 which I wish now that I'd kept. It was actually much newer than my last car and I still had a few grand left over.

In the meantime, and this is where the grassing up comes into my story. It turns out that another doorman who is still a good friend of mine, but is a man to be reckoned with, quite a violent man when he wants to be. Well, the lorry, which it turns out was stolen from Tilbury Docks, was owned by a friend of his. This friend says to him, "Try and get the load back for me." Of course, it creeps through the grapevine that these two other doormen had stolen it. So, he goes to visit them at their place and says, "I know you took the wine but, who did you sell it to?"

They don't tell him until he threw petrol over one of them and threatened to torch him, which he would have done. So, I don't blame him for grassing me up. One of them said, "I sold it to Ronnie Buckingham."

Then of course I got a phone call from this particular guy. Now I got on well with him. He said, "I think we need to have a meet Ron." I said, "Yeah ok, that's how it is." We met up somewhere, I believe it was at one of those Little Chefs. I thought, "Oh I don't need this." This guy, he was a handful.

He didn't frighten me, and I definitely didn't frighten him. When I got there, I said to him, "Look mate, the load's gone." He wanted me to get it back, but I said, "How can I? I don't sell it off and then go begging it back again, it's gone." I told him I didn't know it had anything to do with him or his pal. It was just me, I bought it and I sold it, end of. I told him I didn't want to fall out with him over it, but the truth is it's gone.

He shook my hand and said, "I understand mate, no problem. However, he went back and took my original car off the other two who had stolen the lorry in the first place. I think the lorry owner claimed on the insurance so he might have even come out in front.

I never blamed the other two, the one who got petrol poured over him has since sadly passed over. He was a lovely, lovely fella. They phoned me and apologised and said to me, "Sorry but we had to put the other fella onto you as he was cutting up really nasty about it." As for me and him, we have still remained good friends.

When I was 65, a crowd of us went out and we all met up in a big Indian Restaurant. It was all of us old doormen. I was mucking about that night with him, as he still runs door. He's probably 15 years younger than me, and still a tough nut. I said to him that night, "Look I'm having it a bit hard, could you give me some work back on the doors?" Straight away he said, "When do you want to start?" I laughed, saying, "You're joking? I'm a fucking old man these days!" He told me, "Mate, I know the strength of you. I'd much rather work with an older fella who I know is going to stand his ground than I would some of these young 'uns who keep running away." I was really, really chuffed by that. To this day we still often laugh about the truck full of wine.

Coming back to my health, I've had to visit a chiropractor over the years and as I've explained, sometimes even when I go to have some treatment on myself, I'm still giving readings.

Here are some words from Marcel...

I have always been very sceptical about this industry and still struggle to appreciate how this works and how this information is relayed to him, I have to concede that this is a very special gift and has been used to help many people over the years. I cannot tell you how many times I have had patients tell me that they have been to see this medium,

Ronnie Buckingham, either one to one or at a show and he has had someone come through and this has given an incredible amount of comfort or closure.

So, I have given up trying to understand it and just accept it as an amazing gift that has helped many people and their loved ones.

I have known Ronnie Buckingham for several years as he is a patient at our chiropractic clinic in Braintree.

I had heard about Ronnie's mediumship and abilities but was somewhat sceptical and a disbeliever but nonetheless intrigued as I had heard reports from people who had received readings from Ronnie and the accuracy of these readings was amazing.

On an occasion several years ago at the end of a treatment session Ronnie was very grateful and asked if there was anything thing that he could do for me as I had managed to make time to see him on a busy Saturday morning.

I explained that there was no need but as a close family member had recently suffered a severe horse-riding accident, I would appreciate it if he could use his "voodoo" to help them out. He was intrigued and started asking questions about this person and then suddenly remarked that I had lost someone close to me that I was fond of, and he suggested that it may have been an uncle.

I assured him that my uncle was still alive and in his 80's. He responded by telling me "No, this is a young man. It is involving a big vehicle, something like an American car". He couldn't make it out initially and I could only think of a friend of mine who died when we were 18 and he was driving a VW Beetle. He was adamant that it was a large vehicle, but he could not make it out and said it was something big and there were a lot of people involved.

At this point I realised that he must be talking about my brother-in-law who died in the Paddington train crash in 1999. 31 people died and many more were injured. I did not mention the accident but said that I thought he was talking about my brother-in-law. He said that he had 2 initials "J" and "D". My brother-in-law's name was Derek John. He explained that he won't always get the exact order of names but wanted to know if we were talking about my sister's husband. I told him that it was my Wife's brother at which point he stopped and said, "tell your wife to come and see me".

She did have a reading some months later and he offered all sorts of very accurate information about her, us and the family.

He even described the house that we were looking at buying but were uncertain about and he reassured her that it was the right decision and that her mom was going to live with us and that her late father was very happy with our plans.

On another occasion, whilst we were completing a building project on our house, I had said to my wife in the morning that I needed to speak to the builder as one of the down pipes wasn't straight and whilst not a big problem it will annoy me. I spoke to the builder on my way out and he agreed and was going to sort it that day. When I got to work Ronnie was one of my patients that morning and he asked how everything was going at our new house (the one he mentioned to wife at her reading).

I explained that we were finishing up a building project. He mentioned, unprompted, that there was something there that need to be corrected and I must not leave it as it was going to annoy me. Almost word for word what I said to my wife that morning.

Best wishes

Marcel

CHAPTER 9

HUSBANDS

Me and my husband were in the audience at the Headgate Theatre in Colchester and to be honest we thought the people Ronnie gave messages to were 'plants.' Maybe it's because it was in a theatre setting and not our own spiritualist church at Fennings Chase, of which my husband is President and I am the Medium Secretary.

Near the end Ronnie said to the audience, "I have someone who suffered a heart attack and didn't pass straight away." My late husband suffered a heart attack and was on life support for six days. I sat there in the darkness waiting for someone to put their hand up. No one did. So, I whispered to AJ my new husband, who I was sitting with, "Shall I shout out?" He told me, "Yes."

Ronnie carried on saying, Would you accept the name Peter?" It was my late husband's name. He told me that he had a motorbike. I said, "Yes, he used to be in the Coggeshall Bastards motorbike group."

He went on to mention our children, saying that one of our children was having a hard time. This was very true as she was missing her dad dreadfully.

Ronnie said that Pete and I had had our time and that he was happy that I had met and married AJ.

The thing that made us really go 'Wow!' was a few days before we saw him, AJ and me had a conversation about me taking Pete's photos down, especially a big one on the stairs at home. Ronnie pointed at AJ and said that Pete, "Admired you as you told her not to take his photos down." Him [AJ] and me were the only ones who knew about this conversation.

I had been asking Pete, in my mind, things like, is it ok to be with AJ? As it felt like I was being disloyal.

I took great comfort in Ronnie's messages as he answered all my questions that evening. I came up to him after and told him just that. All I want to say is thank you Ronnie, you are an amazing medium.

Take care

Love Sharon and AJ x

I have been coming to see Ronnie now for over nine years, ever since my husband passed from this world. In the beginning, I was beyond devastated, an emotional wreck. He has given me more comfort, peace and hope than anyone else has ever been able to. I have read that a good medium should be able to pick up on about eight to ten things that they would have no knowledge of in a 45-minute reading to prove their authenticity.

I have eleven tapes of my readings with Ronnie. I can honestly say that on every single tape he has told me 40 to 50 things that he could never know. Ronnie's accuracy is astonishing, and he never ceases to amaze me with what he has told me, some of which nobody on earth, except my husband and myself would know. Ronnie has given me proof and reassurance that my husband is happy and waiting for me to join him when my time comes. That is the most precious gift to be able to bestow on someone.

Thank you is such an inadequate word for everything you have given me and done for me Ronnie, but it's the only word I know. I'm grateful every day for your incredible gift, your compassion and the fact that I'm fortunate enough to have you in my life.

Wishing you all the best of everything,

Libby

Easter day 2009 my amazing husband passed away after a brave fight with pancreatic cancer and cancer of the oesophagus. My daughters at the time were just three and four years old. Michael was diagnosed terminally ill in 2006 when the girls were only one and two years old and he was given 3-6 months to live. At that time, we were already engaged and had planned to be married in 2007. We were advised, if we wanted to marry, to bring our wedding day forward as they didn't believe he would still be with us on our planned wedding day (his birthday the following year) so we changed it to my birthday 17th September 2006.

Michael refused to give up and fought the battle for as long as he could but unfortunately succumbed on Easter day 12th April 2009. As you can imagine, I felt utterly lost.

Two young children and I felt like, even though we had the time, there were certain things we didn't discuss. Basically, it was because both of us were living for the day and making the most of the time we still had together as a family.

A couple of months after Micheal's passing away, my friend Carol, who had previously sought comfort many times from different spiritualists, mentioned Ronnie's name to me. We found out he was doing an evening in Halstead at I believe the Mill. The idea was to go there and have a meal and the possibility, if chosen, a reading too. I remember being sat at the table, the anxiety I felt was immense.

I was still feeling Michael's presence with me, in my heart. I was desperate for a message, but I was trying my hardest not to get too worked up at the same time.

Mick with his dog Bobby

The very first reading of the night it was my Mick who came through!!! Ronnie described him to a tee. He said how he had passed, and described the circumstances, how it had happened. I remember Ronnie told me where his ashes were at the time and the complications there were with the family over his ashes too. Ronnie also told me how many photos there were of him on my fridge (at the time I could not confirm this was true.)

However, I went home and went straight to the fridge and Ronnie was, once again, spot on. He described Mick's van (turquoise blue and yellow.... not your normal colour van), it was sat on the drive with no tax and insurance.

I could never drive it, but I was scared to get rid of it. Ronnie told me, "He's saying, let it go!"

That particular part of the message for me was massive. Ronnie went on to mention our boy (our dog Bobby) and how, "Michael will be waiting for him." Bobby is now 16 years old, 17 this year. I still feel comforted knowing that, when the day comes, I have confirmation that Mick is there waiting for his little boy.

Ronnie also mentioned that Mick said he watches the girls at night but does not want to scare them. I had a babysitter who at that time said she saw a figure walk along the landing once the girls were in bed. He also told me, "I can see him in the woods with a carrier bag walking your dog (Bobby)". Mick used to take a carrier bag into the woods to collect chestnuts on a dog walk!

This was my first experience of seeing Ronnie Buckingham and from that day onwards my belief was 100% in the spiritual world. I genuinely believe there are very few and far gifted people like Ronnie. I've made sure I make some time to come to one of his evenings at least once a year ever since. I have had many other very accurate messages through from Ronnie since then but that first experience will never be beaten!

He is amazing and does an amazing thing and brings so much comfort to people that need it.

Kind regards

Becky x

I saw Ronnie, must be about 20 years ago in Pinewoods Pub in Collier Row, which incidentally isn't there anymore. At the time I was a young widow with two young daughters. My husband came through and I was blown away with what Ronnie told me. He was so accurate with everything he said. The biggest thing being that I had recently had my kitchen, not only redecorated, but a wall knocked down and another one put up elsewhere. Ronnie said, "Your husband doesn't recognise the kitchen." He also said that my husband was asking where have all the magnets gone. The old fridge freezer was full of magnets but when I got the new one, most of the magnets were taken down. Again, this just blew me away.

Another thing Ronnie said to me was that my husband was talking about the Isle of Wight. When we were getting married, we didn't have money to go on a honeymoon, as we were in the process of buying a brand-new house as well as paying for the wedding. One day, while I was at work, my then fiancé phoned me to say that he had booked a honeymoon to the Isle of Wight! Again, this blew me away.

There was quite a bit of information Ronnie gave me that night to reassure me that there is most definitely a spiritual world out there. After all, how would he have known all this information? At the end of the evening the friends I was with were chatting with him. I stood back but Ronnie spoke directly to me saying, "You got a lot from tonight." I have to say I most certainly did.

It gave me so much peace knowing my beloved husband was close by. Thank you Ronnie, for giving me peace.

With regards,

Caroline

Ronnie helped to end the 42 years of torment and hell that I had been living. I came to see one of his shows at Colchester Rugby club about a year ago. I had spent those 42 years visiting different psychics and mediums to find out if my husband, who was tragically killed, blamed and hated me for everything around his death and the years following.

No one had ever been able to get through to my husband until I met Ronnie

Nobody had ever been able to get him through until I met Ronnie at that show. My husband came straight through to Ronnie. Afterwards Ronnie kindly offered me a private reading to tell me more. During that private reading he was able to tell me so much and totally gave me peace for the first time since my husband's death.

I also found one of Ronnie's meditations [guided spirit walks.] I have never been able to meditate or relax before, but that [virtual] walk along the beach was the most amazing thing ever. All my dear departed family were at the end of the beach with my beautiful husband. Oh, my goodness! The tears are flowing down my face now as I write this, just remembering it. My husband stepped forward and *embraced me with so much love. We hugged and held each other until Ronnie's voice told me I had to leave and walk back along the beach. That was so hard to leave him, but I knew I must. I kept looking back 'til I was too far away to see them.*

That journey was my final confirmation of all Ronnie had told me. My husband was there and still loves and cares for me and our boys, as he did the day he was killed. Finally, I can rest and be at peace again after so many years of turmoil and hell.

I can't put into words what you have done for me Ronnie. You are an amazing, kind and generous man and you have given me a life again. I 100% know my husband will be there waiting for us when our time comes.

Thank you, thank you, thank you.

Bev Burton x

What Bev was describing above was her experience of one of my Guided Spirit Walks, which is a form of meditation. A lot of people say I have a very reassuring voice. Basically, what I do is I tell people to go to a quiet place and to listen to what I say. I tell people to feel things and to visualise things in their minds with their eyes closed. I actually do several versions of spirit walks.

One where you get into a hot air balloon. This one mentioned by Bev, where you walk along the beach and the final one I do is on a river. With the beach one I start off by putting people at their ease. I say something like, depending on their circumstances, if you've got kids they are being looked after. You don't have any worries at all. The whole day is yours, you haven't got to go home to make food, and just yours alone.

You're staying on your own, you're in a guest house, you sleep then you get up and have a bit of breakfast, outside it's lovely and sunny etc.

Next, I tell people to go barefoot. I explain that they are on a pavement where the tarmac is nice and warm and then they slowly walk across the road, checking that there are no cars coming. I take them off the pavement onto steps which lead them onto a sandy beach. I get them to feel each of the steps before the beach and introduce the feeling of each of the steps. Next, they are walking along soft, warm sand by the water's edge. As we walk along climbing over the wooden groynes along the beach getting them to really feel each of the different surfaces. Eventually I say to them there are people you can see in the distance. I get them to visualise walking towards these people. I tell them, you know them, but you don't know how you know them. I tell them that they feel drawn to them and then I leave them. I give them about 15 minutes and then I come back with my voice saying, "Right it's time for us to go now."

The feedback from these guided spirit walks has been absolutely phenomenal. It has brought so much comfort to people. I've done them before during a workshop for people. They've come out of them just silently sobbing. The technique puts you in the right frame of mind to see your departed loved ones again.

You can also see Ronnie doing one of his Guided Spirit Walks on YouTube following this link:
https://www.youtube.com/watch?v=iqTiUGtSGlw

Nicky and I went on holiday to Tenerife. One night Nicky got up and was dancing with these two older women as Nicky loves to dance. I don't dance but she loves to. Before she'd joined them both on the dance floor I'd said to Nicky about them. I told her they'd both lost their husbands. As she's dancing with them, they were talking about the fact that they'd lost their husbands and Nicky told them, "I know." They said how do you know? So, Nicky told them that her husband was a Medium. She said that I'd told her about both of them before she started dancing.

Before she'd got up to go over to join them, I'd told Nicky, one of the women won't have anything to do with mediumship but the other one I pointed to her and I said, "That lady, her heart is breaking over losing her husband."

I think her name was Betty. After they came off the dance floor, she came over to me to ask about what I'd said. I said to Nicky. So, I said, "Let's go somewhere quieter." I sat with her, and I held her hand and I said, "He's wearing a golfing shirt, a green one and it's got captain written on it" It turned out that these ladies came from Liverpool and he was, when he was alive, captain of his golf club. I said to her, "Would you accept the name John?" and she confirmed that's him, that was his name. I told her about the kids, the fact that they had two. Then I said to her "Can I put my arm round you, as he wants me to demonstrate something." She said, "Yes of course." So, I put my arm around her and I made a clicking noise with my teeth, saying "You're still my girl"

At that moment she just broke down in tears. She told me that when he was alive, every night, for all of their married life, when they got into bed he would always put his arm around her and make that sound and say those exact words. She was in bits. She said to Nicky, "How on earth could Ronnie know that?

That is unbelievable." She turned to me and said, "You actually made the sound he always made, that little click, as well as saying his exact phrase."

CHAPTER 10

A PICTURE PAINTS A THOUSAND WORDS

You might be wondering about my book cover for this latest book and the painting of me on the front. It was done by the artist called James Wilkinson. James is famous for his pop art which has taken him on tour with the Rolling Stones and also in many other directions including teaching, staging exhibitions, charity fundraising, curating, collecting and, most recently, opening a gallery.

His main painting muse has been music. James has painted a galaxy of stars, including David Bowie, Ed Sheeran, Tinie Tempah, Amy Winehouse, George Ezra, Jools Holland, and the Rolling Stones. You can see some of his works in Friars Street, Sudbury in Suffolk at Pop Nouveau, an art gallery that celebrates the talent, skill and imagination behind the album covers and promotional material. You can also find out more about the gallery via this link https://popnouveau.co.uk/

Here is James's story…

My art studio is at the historic Highlands House in Chelmsford. I have been interested in painting the supernatural for years. I have seen Coral Polge [a dedicated spirit artist for 54 years, passing to spirit in 2001. She was able to create portraits of loved ones in the spirit world] at the SAGB [Spiritualist Association of Great Britain] when I was in my early twenties. She gave me a portrait which turned out to be my friend's sister who died and who I had never met.

I've painted the ghost that haunts Highlands House through witness statements in a kind of 'police photo-fit' way. Listening to their testimonials, I had just completed a huge portrait of Vanessa Mitchell, owner of The Cage, the witches' prison in St. Osyth. So I decided that I'd like to paint a Medium. I started asking around and the name that kept coming up was Ronnie Buckingham, with glowing reports on his ability.

Ever the sceptic, I decided to attend a local demonstration that he was doing near Braintree and I sat and watched.

I'd seen a lot of so-called 'superstar mediums,' including Doris Stokes, and I felt that nine out of ten of them were useless in my opinion. Ronnie, however, had a much more open and honest way about him and I was impressed by his hit rate. After the demonstration, I approached his daughter and asked if it would be possible to get Ronnie to sit for his portrait. I was introduced to Ronnie, and we hit it off straight away.

However, I was honest about my scepticism and Ronnie respected that. We have to this day, an understanding that he only has to tell me one thing to make me believe totally, however in the meantime, I can confirm Ronnie has rattled off names and nicknames of far-off people and family members that he simply could not have known.

Ronnie came to my home for the sitting and we got down to do business. We agreed on a pose that I had in mind. I decided on this particular pose, as I know Ronnie likes to touch the person's hand when he contacts the other side. After the photos were taken for my reference, I asked Ronnie if he'd stay for lunch. I had also invited my best friend's recently widowed wife to join us. She was staying with us, and Ronnie had no idea that she was in the house. As soon as she walked in, he said to her "You're the reason I'm here today." He proceeded to tell her pretty much everything that confirmed her late husband Chris was still with us.

Ronnie and I have stayed friends ever since and I'm hoping we get to work on some exciting projects in the future. I think Ronnie has a special gift and one day he might be able to tell me the one thing that I need to know.

James

The reason for writing this second book was that, by 2016 and before then I'd become well known but very few people knew about my checkered and rather troubled past. I felt it was better for me to say it, rather than for someone to put it out on Facebook one day saying, "Oh I knew Ronnie when he was in prison!"

Also, if you've read *Medium Rare*, you'll know that I also mentioned in my first book about leopards changing their spots. I can honestly say one million percent that I have changed over the years. I wouldn't do one fraction of the things I'm doing nowadays years ago, if any of them really. In those days I was getting into fights, criminality, and that sort of thing. I wanted also to let people know that you could be, I suppose, a 'bad person' if that's the right word, man or woman and still end up turning the corner and doing something good with your life.

This second book of mine, it's now more important than ever before to prove life after death. I want to take away the fear for my readers that you will never see your loved ones again. Don't get me wrong, no one can take away the physical pain of loss from a bereavement. However, when you do pass on you continue to watch over your loved ones.

With the feedback I got from my first book, *Medium Rare*, people were screaming out for me to write another book. There are still people who want to know and hear about proof of the afterlife through my readings with individuals. That's why this book is full of brand-new true-life accounts from people I've read for, whether on a one-to-one basis or as part of an organised event.

I just want to make a few points at this junction in the book about being labelled as an International Medium or a Celebrity Medium. Those are two labels I don't really like when it comes to describing what I do and who I am. A title like International Medium means nothing.

You can be a terrible Medium and work overseas and therefore call yourself an International Medium. Then you can give readings which are just as bad as they are in the UK.

Years ago, when I was very popular and appearing on TV, I was working for people. They would advertise me as Ronnie Buckingham International Medium. I would always make light of it with a joke saying I'm actually an Eastern National (Medium as I came by bus. Some mediums, it's true will go out of their way to seek out the celebrities and then try and get them to one side and give them a message. I've read celebrities too but not by doing that.

Me with Boxer Steve Collins

I described earlier that I was invited to go to Manchester to meet several celebrities who wanted readings. I went to the Reading Rooms there and I also got to meet the boxer Steve Collins and read for him. He actually did a video of me.

When I did Mystic Challenge on the TV I met a lot of celebrities there too.

You had a jury of 12 people, basically you had mystics, psychics, palm readers, tarot readers and it was a challenge to see who would come out on top. The mystery celebrity would come into the room. You were challenged with doing a reading with them but you couldn't see them, they had like a big white hood on and you could only see their eyes and their hands. Some even wore gloves and they weren't allowed to say a word to you. You had someone else in the room too to officiate and they would either do shorthand of what you said or they taped you. The studio gave you 20 minutes to either read their cards or do whatever.

I'd hold their hand, and that's how I'd pick up on the person. I can't remember them all as it was so long ago. However, one day I do remember I was up against a very good lady but they chose me as the winner of this particular episode. The celebrity guest turned out to be the Reverend Lionel Fanthorpe. Lionel actually said to the producer of that episode, "That man that read me, I saw his eyes and he's a beautiful, beautiful soul." I remember thinking, "Wow!"

Lionel Fanthorpe is a TV presenter, author, Anglian priest and he rides a Harley Davidson, plus he did martial arts as well. I said he was a religious man who was one of five children and that he came from the East End of London. He worked in a scrapyard. Paul Ross the presenter used to say to the others I was up against, each that they'd got their work cut out that day as they were up against, Medium Ronnie Buckingham.

All of the crew used to also come to me for readings. One day a chap a palmist, Ian I think his name is, very, very good, he used to work in Selfridges, just a great palmist. When we were going down in the lift together to go on to the set, he said to me, "I can't beat you, you're the best that there is." I did beat him on that day too.

The way it worked was they'd put you in a room with the celebrity who was covered up and not allowed to speak. There would also be a chaperone in the room with you both and you got say 20 minutes with them. Then they put you in a box, with another person to check that you couldn't hear or see anything while Paul Ross the presenter would talk to the now uncovered celebrity and tell the audience about them.

Then they call you out and that's the first time you realise who the celebrity is. You'd say to Paul Ross what you thought your best hits were and you had only 90 seconds to tell him. Then they'd do the same with the other person you were up against and then a jury with a head judge, normally a journalist from the National press, would decide who got most right answers on the day.

Mystic Challenge was on Sky TV and as I said it was hosted by Paul Ross. I read him too and predicted that he'd leave his wife and meet someone else, which he did. You filmed three shows a day. I was really nervous as it was TV. Uri Geller was on the panel at the time. I'd always wanted to meet him and there was an advert I saw saying if you'd like to be on the show etc. so I phoned up to ask if I could be a judge on the show. The lady I spoke to said, "Have you got any knowledge of that sort of thing?"

So, I told her I was a working medium. She told me they were looking for people to be in the show.

She said to me, "Would you be willing to come to London and pass a psychic test?" I told her no as I was busy working. So, she said, "Could you read someone over the phone? They can't speak to you but I'm going to pass the phone over to someone now, I'll give you a moment to tune in and see what you can do."

I think the lady I did the reading for over the phone that day her name was Diane Cooper. I got her mum through, and it absolutely blew her away and so they asked me to come on the following week! I remember the night before I said to Nicky, I dreamt that one of the people I was to read will be a jockey. It turned out to be the 'Rastafarian showjumper and actor' Oliver Skeete and he was the first person I read on the show.

When I told the producers what I'd said to Nicky before I left that morning, they rang her up and asked her to confirm it which of course she did. I didn't win that episode. I took part in all in 15 shows, I won 12 of them lost 2 and I drew one as well.

There is still an episode you can watch on YouTube via this link https://www.youtube.com/watch?v=aZ6S8rWExlk with guest star Adrian Doughty who is a cabaret star and one of the Balloon Dancing Men.

Don't get me wrong, I'm not one to chase celebrities. I have been featured in many magazines over the years. One in particular, Spirit & Destiny Magazine, the editor phoned me up as she was so astounded by my reading.

Spirit & Destiny Magazine who featured me regularly

For this magazine I would be sent some photographs of people, but nothing else. No names or dates or details. Just the picture. I would look at them and then send them the information I'd got through from the spirit world about the picture. One of them was a picture of a young woman.

I said that her name began with an S and ended in an A, like Sara or Susanna. I said that she was a Taurian and in the medical field like a doctor's receptionist. I said when she writes her address the word Heath is in it. The name Peter or Petra runs right through her family. I said that she suffered with varicose veins and that she'd just broken up with someone who rides a motorbike and that she was raped in London last year by two men.

After I'd sent in the information to the magazine the Editor rang me absolutely gobsmacked to say that it was all absolutely true. The woman whose picture it was, didn't want the fact she'd been raped to be put into print which was fair enough. The Editor said to me that day, "How can anyone tell all of that from a photograph?" I did lots of pictures just like that for this particular magazine over several months.

Another magazine got me to hold people's diaries which were all sealed in envelopes. I actually got, not just the first name of the diary owner, but the whole name of the person who wrote the diary on that occasion. I remember another of the diaries I said, everything in this diary is just Adam and the Ants. When they opened it up, it was a schoolgirl's diary and she'd written I love Adam and the Ants all over it.

I can't explain it to people but it's like I can put myself into a different realm and I can just see things that other people can't. Because I don't look like that sort of man, people find it hard to believe that I have this gift. When you see me for the first time you are going to make an assumption of what you think I look like, maybe a bouncer, or yob! Let's face it, I'm not a typical Medium that people have come to expect.

Another time I remember I was doing readings in Norfolk. I was there with a spiritualist church giving messages for charity. I did a reading with a gay guy called Mike. His mother had always loved him regardless of his sexuality, but his father had disowned him.

As I was reading for him, I kept getting the words, "Oooo Mrs!" coming through to me. And I thought that sounds like Frankie Howard. To be honest, to start with I kind of dismissed it. In my mind I thought what would the real

Frankie Howard want with him? It kept getting louder and louder, the same phrase over and over. So, I said to him, "Look I know you're going to think I'm mad, but I've got Frankie Howard here and he wants to talk to you." That's when he told me that he'd actually lived with Frankie for three years.

They were fellow thespians. Frankie Howard meant the world to him. So that also meant a lot to me, to have him come through, as I really liked Frankie Howard when he was on this side of life.

At the end of the day a celebrity is just a person like you or I. I tend not to say much about my so-called Celebrity readings for that very reason. They are people who love and lose just the same as we do.

People say to me are you happy doing the job you do, i.e. mediumship. I have to say I am happier now than I have ever been in my entire life. Way back when I was working the doors as a doorman in my 20s and 30s and even some of my 40s, I worked at the Windmill in Colchester and I had some great friends. Yes, I had some good times then too. It was always a laugh and there were always loads of women and music. Plenty of camaraderie among us door men too and I do sometimes miss that.

All of them great friends, some who have sadly passed but those who are still here, remain great friends to this day. I was lucky in the clubs that I worked at. There was always cabarets going on and let's just say it wasn't a great life for a married man but at the time wonderful memories. I remember when I left working on the doors in the year 2000. Actually, it was the very end of 1999 just before the turn of the new millennium. A particular chap that I worked with at the time was 6ft 4ins and built like a brick shite house. He was my Jamaican friend I mentioned in Chapter 5 Roy Stuart. When I was on telly people would go up to the Windmill where I worked and say to him, "Hey Roy, that mate Ronnie of yours, have you seen what he's doing now?" Roy would say to them, "Listen, if you're gonna cuss the man go do it somewhere else. Don't say anything bad about the man in front of me, or you'll find there's a problem!"

As I mentioned earlier, Roy is now living in Tenerife, and I've popped over to see him there. We still call each other regularly and we call each other 'Brothers from a different Mother.' I'm still in touch with him now, all those years later. Some of the other mates I had on the doors included, John Carrell, Colin (Bolchie), Kieran White, Scott Gray, Pete Townswell and several others who I'm still in touch with. Many of those sadly we've lost including Timmy H, Kevin Keeshan, Shaun Spooner, Pete Spencer Mick McCabe, Micky Burridge, Sean Harris and Ted Stibble all good friends who have now sadly passed on. Ultimately working the doors, it's still a young man's job.

However nowadays I get so much more enjoyment and satisfaction out of giving readings and being able to help people with their losses. The readings I deliver give me a great deal of self-worth these days. If I had to choose between being a medium or working the doors I would choose what I'm doing now without a doubt.

When I had my knee operated on the first time, it made me feel very, very low. I joined a site for people who had had total knee replacements. It was marvelous for me because you could see that other people had gone through what you were going through. They were also having the same setbacks and the same frustrations. When someone passes over to the other side, I hope that the bereaved person will read some of the true accounts and experiences of another bereaved person I've read for in this book and from reading those messages it might just turn their life around and give them hope. That's what I really hope happens with this book.

CHAPTER 11

A GRANDPARENT'S WISDOM

Years ago, I too went for a reading with a chap called Barry Lee in Clacton. I went with a mate of mine Micky Tingy. Micky went in first and he came out in tears. He said, "Bloody hell! Jack came through!" (a mate we'd lost who was Greek.) Jack was a bit of a chap, always had his shirt sleeves rolled up to show off his arms. Well, he came through to Micky via the medium that day. Jack told the medium that he hit a tree in a forest, which he did. He was driving back to Woodford in Essex driving from Epping and he fell asleep at the wheel. Jack was tough when he was alive and he told the medium, "It don't matter how tough you are on earth, it don't matter up here. It's a different world."

So, I went in next and the medium was also very good with me. He picked my grandad up straight away, telling me that he was a very violent man. Which was correct, he was an ex-professional boxer, and he was also a violent man out of the ring. The medium gave my parents a bad mark up. He told me, "You're a young man who had to grow up very quickly and learn to do things on your own."

He told me back then that I didn't know where I was going in life but that I would eventually get there. At the time I was lodging with a mate as I'd broken up with my first wife. I did drive a nice car, so I pulled up outside his house in a white BMW. I was wearing a nice Burberry cardigan, and I didn't have a lot but you couldn't tell as I looked alright. Straight away he told me, "You're sleeping out of suitcases. You're drifting from one house to another house." Which was all true.

Me with Medium Anne Walmsley a great friend who helped launch my career

So it was that experience which interested me in mediumship. Then, as I talked about in my first book *Medium Rare*, I saw a spirit in my bedroom at the foot of my bed. It was the ghost of a man and I saw him disappear into the wall opposite us. So, I also knew there was something in this 'life after death' people talked about.

It fascinated me but I certainly didn't know that I had the gift back then. I had to have all of these life experiences first and the gift lay dormant in me.

When it did come along, it came along so quickly. In my first year I worked in front of 1000 people.

I was invited to do a demonstration for Cawston College in Norfolk. It was an old school, owned by a chap called Steve Barry with the backing of some Swiss People.

Together they turned it into the UKs first ever psychic hotel.

With Margaret Patterson you can see a spirit forming next to me! It wasn't the sun as that was in front of us that day.

I was told it normally takes years to get to that standard. I just found that I could read people very accurately from day one. So, from the old days to now all I can say is Wow! What a change.

It took me a long while to accept this gift. I spent many months thinking but why me? Why give me this gift and not someone else more deserving of it. I've hurt a few people physically, over my life and I've broken a few hearts. Saying that I've had my heart broken a few times too! Let's just say I was a bit of a sod, a bit of a player in my time with the ladies. I was a thief and I've been to prison. It sounds funny to say this but I've always, all my life, had morals. Sounds daft now you're reading about my past.

If I'm driving past a little old lady struggling, I'll always stop the car and go and help her.

If I'm at an ice cream van and I see snotty nosed kids there who can't afford one, I'll buy them all an ice cream. I've always been like that. I've always been polite, I mean, I do swear, but I'll always open doors for ladies and say please and thank you.

Nicky always says that when I go out my manners are impeccable. I'm old school like that. I also don't like bullies. If I've hit someone way back in my past, then they've asked for it. I've never done bullying. When I worked on the doors, and I had to throw someone out I'd always try to talk them out of it first. If they got a clump, then they got a clump. I would regularly ask the spirit world, why give me the gift when there are people out there who, in my mind, were more spiritual than me.

I do think however, that you've got to be fearless to be a good medium. You've got to be able to say things that not everyone likes. For example, and of course I won't name names here but, I have said to a lady, "I've got your son here. Now I know you loved him and all that, but your son was not a nice fella. He was a nasty piece of work. He took drugs, he drank, and he knocked his wife about." You've got to tell it how it is. A lot of other mediums would pull back from that. How deep it goes perhaps depends on what you're willing to say. I just put it out there. Everyone says to me that I'm the most point blank, tell it how it is, medium on the circuit. They are right, that's just how I am. I will pull people up on things. If there's bad news, I'll give them bad news. If things aren't right, I'll let them know that.

Another thing that I try to explain to people is that when you go across to the other side, you don't grow wings and become a saint. You come back to me, as the medium, as you were when you were living. So, if someone was violent and nasty on earth, I'll know it as I'll be able to sense that about their spirit.

If I said, "Oh I have someone's dad here and what a lovely man!" Yet the reality was that he actually used to kick the dog and beat his wife up, the person I'm addressing would say well sorry but that's not my dad. However, if I'm honest about him warts and all then they know and recognise that it's their dad.

Sometimes I can see a change in the person, and I can say that in the reading. I can say, "Well he's mellowed a bit during his time over there." Other times I'll sense that they are not regretful about the way they lived their life and I have to be honest about that too.

The way I understand it you get a chance up there to look back over your life. To look back over all of the hurt you've caused but also all of the love you've given. I think bad deeds are weighed up against good deeds. Personally, I've done a lot of bad things, but I know that I've done a lot more good things now with my life. I just love the gift I've got I really do. I don't think I've got an ego with it, at least I don't believe so. I've seen a lot of not very good mediums who it's all about 'Look at me, I can do this amazing thing.'

For me a real gift is like the chap who painted the picture of me which I've used for my front cover of this book – that to me is a real gift. What I've got doesn't make me any better than anyone else. If you said to me, come and fix this plug or cut a plank of wood – I'm fucking useless! I have to pay people to do DIY for me. I've just got this niche and I'm good at what I do. I can say that I'm always thankful for it as it changed my life for the better. I'm a happier man nowadays too.

Now don't get me wrong, when I was young, I was fit, strong and I had hair! I was on the ball but inside I wasn't happy. In those days I was never the best at anything. I was a good weightlifter, a good bodybuilder, I could fight but I wasn't the best fighter. Now I don't think there are many mediums out there who are better than myself. There may be a few but I know that I'm up there amongst the best of the best. I know that. I've had enough people tell me. Because of that it has changed my views on things too.

When you're a thief you have a 'thieves' eye' you can't change that. Back in the day if we went into a shop, straightway you'd notice their safe. You'd be looking to see if the shop was alarmed up, had security cameras etc. You're always looking to steal. You might notice a car pull up outside a jewellers and someone getting out with a briefcase. Straightaway you're thinking are they going in there? I bet he's carrying gold in there. In that case, we'll follow him and see what happens. You think, maybe if he leaves the car, when he's gone, we'll break into it and see what he's left in there.

Now I don't look. I don't see it anymore. I think I've gone the other way. I hate mugging, if I see someone looking like they're going to mug someone, now I'd have to steam in there to stop them. I also don't like drugs. It's something I never touched. Stealing off your own is not the thing to do. No stealing is correct, but you do feel better stealing off those who can afford it!

In those days if you broke into a warehouse or maybe a jewellers or if you robbed a post office to me it would be, Fuck 'em! It ain't their money. Of course, it's wrong but that's how you justify it in your mind at the time. Another thief once said to me, "Have you noticed how anyone we rob from, they're always 'orrible bastards! They always deserve it." If you robbed a book maker you'd say, "Oh he was a nasty bastard anyway, so he deserved it!" The truth was he was probably a really nice fella. That's what I did back then, in those days. I would continually make excuses for myself.

100% I feel very different now as a person. There was always a nicer side to me. I've had men come through to me during a reading who were abusive, but they explained to me to pass onto whoever they were abusive with whilst on earth, that they were brought up with abuse. They knew nothing else. They didn't know any other way to be. I've turned full circle. I'm so gentle now. When Nicky and I first got together I would still rage, that was in me, but not now. I'm cool with it all now. I might still have a little tantrum every now and then but it don't last long.

A lot of that is down to the fact I've not been in the greatest of health in the last couple of years and I'm also suffering from some hearing loss. I just get frustrated with it all sometimes. With the AF I can no longer take part in the big bike rides anymore. I think sometimes, "Would I like to ride another trike?" [a three-wheeled motorbike] These days. I hate wearing crash helmets and you don't have to with a trike.

I used to have a 1000CC one and I used to fly about on it everywhere in my little woolly hat and my sunglasses in a tee shirt. Great times. I probably won't though as if I come off, I'm on blood thinners so I'm gonna bleed out! Or I could injure myself badly and I don't want that. Inside I'm still a young man. I used to also love weightlifting, but I can't lift weights or train like I used to anymore either. I was also a decent golfer, I played off at about nine [handicap]. Thanks to my more recent knee issues I can no longer play golf anymore either. I'm still hoping I might be able to again one day. I've not played now for four years. I used to be a member of a senior's golf team for the over 50's and we used to go out and play all over, including at Felixstowe Ferry Golf Club, and Saffron Walden I loved those courses. So, a lot has been taken away from me.

Here's some more readings where grandparents have shared their wisdom ...

I lost my Nan 10 years ago, and was lucky to get a reading with Ronnie. A few things were mentioned at the reading, the first one being extremely true about a family member. I knew right then that my nan could see it for what it truly was. I played the recording of my reading back to my now ex-partner. He was my partner at the time and my nan had told Ronnie that she wasn't happy with a bloke in my life. I remember at the time thinking perhaps it was my son's dad. Ronnie went onto to say that Nan was saying no she's talking about me. I laughed and said course she's not.

Now the truth has come out and I've listened to that recording over and over again. I know 100% that Ronnie was right, it was my ex-partner that Nan was talking about all along.

Having the reading brought me so much joy. Hearing from my Nan was amazing. Ronnie truly brought me so many happy tears, my nan Edie was my world. I named my little girl after her, so she shines through her always. I still miss her so much but thank you so much for bringing her to me and letting me know she is always around me and my babies.

Keep doing what you're doing, Ronnie you bring so much joy and happiness to so many people. Nan you're the light of the family always.

Faye Barnard

Ronnie, I thought I would tell you my story as I wanted you to know what a massive impact you had on my life. Without exaggeration you changed my life (for the better) and it's nice for me to be able to share that with you. I am just so grateful to you.

I came to see Ronnie when I was approaching a major crossroads in my life. Nothing was going right for me in terms of relationships and work. I was desperate for a baby but couldn't find a man who I felt was 'father material' and time was ticking. Without giving him any information about myself he almost made me fall off my chair with his accuracy. After initially holding my hand, Ronnie fired off information that no one could have known about me unless he had hired a private detective!

Ronnie started off saying that I worked in an office but not just any ordinary office, he could see newspapers flying off a press...wait a minute, he said, "You work for the Essex County Standard." Absolutely correct.

He certainly had my attention now. He had made contact with my nan who told him I wanted to become a mum. Ronnie held my hand again and told me my body was capable of carrying a baby. Then he said to me, "But you already know that, as you have had investigations already." Indeed, I had, at a private fertility clinic. Ronnie told me I would have one successful pregnancy which may result in twins. I was in fact already receiving fertility treatment with a donor.

With regards to my work life, he told me I was in a rut and needed to be brave and make a decision. What he didn't realise was I had been in the job for 20 years and I had the option of taking voluntary redundancy which in fact I needed to fund my fertility journey.

I came out of Ronnie's house with a clear mind for once and felt I now had the confidence to go for what I wanted. It was now or never. The next Monday I went in to work and asked for a meeting with my manager. I told him I wanted to be considered for the next round of redundancies which was just a few weeks away. I left work in April and managed to find another job to keep me going financially in the meantime. The redundancy money gave me the funds for IVF with the donor and I became pregnant in June on my first attempt. I had previously had seven attempts at insemination. Each time I had a failed pregnancy test. I wasn't upset as I focused on what Ronnie had told me and I had the trust and belief that I would become pregnant at some point.

I gave birth to a healthy baby boy the following April after three embryos were implanted. Although 14 embryos were created and frozen they all perished so there was no chance of a later pregnancy. He was right again! I did only have one pregnancy.

Without his reading I don't know if I would have had the confidence to make such a life-changing decision on my own and finally become a mum. My son is almost 14 now and I think about it most days. I dread to think what may have happened if I didn't have my reading with Ronnie that day.

Thank you so much Ronnie

Tracy Hogan

I have a very tall man here, with a curly head of hair

A long time back, probably around the late '90s I joined one of my daughters at an evening with Ronnie in Halstead. It was my first ever, so I wasn't really sure what to expect. After the evening had come to a close, I remember Ronnie was sitting at a table saying goodbye to people as they left. I said to my daughter, "I feel so drawn I need to go over to Ronnie."

So, I did, very shyly. I shook his hand and told him how much I had enjoyed the evening. Ronnie took my hand and cupped it in his own and said, "I have a very tall man here, with a curly head of hair, your dad, no it's your grandad." (I always used to call him dad). He continued, "He says he loves you." I was blown away by this and one day I'll tell Ronnie exactly why. I have treasured those words from that night ever since. Yes, I'm a believer in the afterlife and you rock Ronnie! I would be honoured for you to share this story in your book.

Tina Cole

Where do I start? I can honestly say that from the time many years ago I first set eyes and ears on Ronnie, I never realised it would change my life. My son phoned me up one day to say, "Mum I've just popped in the pub for a pint, and I was asked to buy a ticket." He said, "I only want a beer!"! The person on the door told him there was a demonstration tonight on spiritual contact, so my son grudgingly bought a ticket as he was desperate for a pint. Anyway, he sat at the bar with his pint and then Ronnie came on. Well, it blew him away and he couldn't wait to tell me all about the evening.

Having heard him so excited by this Medium, I booked up for the next one. I drove from Suffolk to Essex with a 7-seater filled with my mates. Once we'd arrived in the pub, as we sat there, I said, "I'm going to get picked" and they all laughed. I said, "I've been told I will", they all thought I was mad. Ronnie looked round the room and then he looked directly at me and started to pick up on my grandad. He said I had a bedroom full of different outfits of what to wear that night, as I kept changing my mind, which was true. He said I had dabbled about a bit with spiritual things but never really got any further. Ronnie told me that night that I needed to trust, and I would succeed.

He also talked about the other side. I learnt a lot that night. One thing that was such a comfort was that I hadn't been this silly little girl, years ago, that imagined all these things. I really had 'seen' people from the age of seven. That night was the start of knowing there really was 'something', I had had all that time which I had wasted as I was an adult now.

So, I booked up to have a one-to-one with Ronnie which was brilliant. I was still a little taken aback and, on the fence, now and again with it all.

His reading was spot on, telling me what I had been through, which truly was a lot, but how I had coped with it all. I did cope from an early age. Always thinking I would be alright but not understanding why I felt like that. I had gone through two rapes, been beaten up by *my first husband and even through all that, I still knew that I would be ok. Somehow, I just knew that it was something I had to go through. Never thinking "Why me? It's not fair!" Just knowing it had to be.*

Weird I know, but after attending some of Ronnie's workshops and my understanding growing more each time, I began to believe more and more. He told me I needed to trust in myself, and I would be a healer and my main purpose was to help others. Later, I had another reading and Ronnie told me my dad was over now, which he was, and would be working with me. He told me that I would be interested in Angels, so I told him then that I thought I had seen one.

Ronnie said I would be a good healer. Since then, I've helped so many people, with both counselling, and have even become a Reiki Practitioner. I also have my own little sideline making crystal bracelets. Up until I met Ronnie, I never believed in myself ever. I was always a dreamer, referred to as 'thick' at school. Now thanks to my son for wanting a pint, and thanks to Ronnie for showing me I can do it, I have got what it takes. I also know that I'm not going mad because I see spirits, work with angels and my lovely dad.

I have become a very special person who helps all sorts, mainly those going through trauma, whether its dealing with rape, or physical abuse, and that's why I needed to experience this, so that I would I know how the victims of these terrible crimes really feel. I help people to heal and I'm never alone. I love my spiritual work, and this truly is all Ronnie's doing.

It was he who I trusted to tell me the truth that I could do this. I know he's always in the background if I needed to ask him something.

For me it also helped to see a 'real man', one from Essex, a tough guy, one who you wouldn't expect would put up with someone who was chatting to spirits! A person who would say it how it is and therefore keeping it real for me.

I thank you Ronnie from my heart as you really helped me to understand that I really 'saw' from the age of seven. Made me make sense of that fact that I needed to suffer for a reason so as to help others, and that I was meant to heal.

Take care, sending love

Sue Risby (Stock) xx

From a Sceptic to Believer: well, where do I begin? I'm not one for spirits and ghosts and all that cobblers, but I've always liked to believe that when your time is up your spirit goes somewhere. I've always thought that you do finally meet up with people that have gone before you. Anyway how this night came about was that my Mrs, Amy had convinced me to go out for a bit of dinner and see a medium at a restaurant. It's a restaurant that I have frequented over the years Marconatos in Hoddesdon. The food's good and the company likewise. Amy said that we were going with our friends Lauren and Bill. Billy is very much like meself, not really a believer in all the spirit stuff. So, I said, "I'll go but I doubt I'll enjoy it." On the way down there in the car I said to the rest, "They're all con merchants, blag artists." Plus a few other choice words!

Amy and Lauren both told me to stop being a 'Misog!' They said, "Just see what happens, you never know what will happen Bill."

Once we'd arrived and sat down at the restaurant, we've had our food and now it's time for this so-called Medium to start his act. So I shot down stairs for a quick wee. As I walked down the stairs I see this big old lump, a bald fella with a few tattoos. He was having a chat with the restaurant Manager. I thought, "He's wondering where this Medium fella is and all, coz he's taking his time." I thought to myself, "I've got work tomorrow!" Anyway, I walked past and I had a wee and I went to go back up the stairs and this bald chap was still there and he made a remark to me. He said, "Hope you boys don't give me no stick up there tonight." I was shocked. I thought, "No way that's him." I went on to think, "Oh yeah, he's definitely a blag artist."

As I walked past him, I thought, "I'll stay quiet and see what it's all about." But then I come back with, "It ain't me you've got to worry about, me mates trouble not me." I left him standing downstairs and I shot up the stairs with me title grin. I remember thinking, "I'm goin to ruin you now." So in he come, made his big entrance throws a few f's and B's about then tells people what they've got to do if they think the message is towards them and let him take the lead.

Ronnie gets goin, a few people in the room relate, then all of a sudden he starts coming up with things about me mate's dad and his brother. Mind-blowing stuff but Bill kept quiet coz he weren't one hundred percent certain. Then Bill had no choice but to put his hand up. Well the rest of what Ronnie said, I was like, "Wow! Nobody could tell me mate the things he was, not without knowing them all their life." It was stuff I didn't even know.

Then he goes on and starts saying, "I've got an old girl here, short, stamp lady, hard faced and she's a greengrocer." I went stone cold. I thought, "Nah, it's not who I think it is." Me Nan, she was a greengrocer. Then Ronnie says, "Her old man's here and he was a Coalman." I froze and the words, "Fuck off!" come straight out me mouth! It was like he was talking about my grandad. Now he described him like he was standing in front of me. He told me he was a very smart man. My grandad wore a collar and tie since I could remember. He was always dapper even if he wasn't goin anywhere. My granddad used to say you never know who could knock on the door. Ronnie told me he was a coal merchant, not just a delivery man. He said that he worked for Fred Ball then later took over the company. He said that he had his own business. Again, all the information about him was spot on. Every word so far was on point and then this is where I got really stunned. Ronnie said, still talking about my grandad, that he would practically give coal away. He said that he would always look after people. Saying, "If their old man was on holiday (banged up) or if they was hard up in the winter he (my grandad) was a gentleman, a well-respected figure in his area." He told me all of this, word for word, on that night.

I burst into tears at this point. Unless you personally knew Thomas Heyman, you couldn't tell me. The stuff he knew about him it's not exactly common knowledge. We were from north London and now we live in Hertfordshire. My grandad was my best mate. He was more of a father than a grandfather. We did everything together. He taught me to ride a bike. Taught me to drive a motor, amongst other things. He moulded me into the man I am today.

Ron kept it short and sweet because he could see I was overwhelmed and in total shock. So, he finished off with, "He still looks out for you know and wants to you to know you couldn't write it." I sat there thinking to myself, "I am a non-believer in all this shit, and he's managed to completely blow me away like that."

Anyway, after the show had finished, I went downstairs as I personally wanted to thank him. I also thought as I walked down the steps, if I needed to hear from anyone, it was me best mate. I thought to myself, that would be the one person, if any, that would make me think it could be real. So, I walked up to Ronnie, and we got talking about a few other things, Freemasonry, ducking and diving, the football and then he said to me, just out the blue, "You've got your grandad's watch haven't you, you kept it." I went cold, I was in total shock again, twice in a matter of hours!

In the left pocket of my jeans was a silver fob watch with my grandad's photo in it. It's something that a very close friend of mine had made for me shortly after I'd lost my grandad. We've got this saying, me and him, Time flies but memories never fade. So, it was a reminder of him that I could carry whenever I wanted. The thing is nobody knew I had the Fob watch with me that particular night, not even my partner knew. I thought to myself, "Fuck me! This fella is warm." That was the icing on the cake for me. At that point my mind was truly made up.

It is true there are people who can talk to the dead and he comes in the shape of a 6ft 3ins bald-headed, ex-crook, out of Hackney - who would of thought it aye?!!

Bill Mahon
Scaffolder from Hertfordshire
(37 years old)

There was a funny spin off in that story above from Billy as last week I was at the Rosey Lea tea rooms in Bishops Stortford doing a demonstration. I got this man come through and in the audience was the wife, the son and his daughter. He was a wonderful man who came through to me. He kept mentioning to me about the Masons. The son said, "My dad wasn't a Mason but I am." Anyway, this chap told me afterwards that he was a sceptic. He actually came to me in tears when the night had finished. Saying, "Mate, Billy told me about you. I'm going to have to tell Bill now that he was right, that you are amazing!" It turns out that he actually knows Billy [Mahon] and that Billy had phoned him up as he knew that he had lost his father. Billy had told him, "You have to go and see Ronnie Buckingham, he's shit hot, he's mustard!"

So, this chap's son looked up where I was next doing an event and he came along with his mum and his sister. Since that night he's also gone onto my waiting list for a one-to-one reading. The chap was called Rico.

Reflecting on my life 13 years ago to the year of 2011, at the young age of 27, times were super tough. Utter heartache consumed me, the future looked bleak, and I struggled to believe that I would ever feel true happiness again. My now ex-husband had left me just after our one-year-old son's birthday and it shook me to the core. I didn't see it coming and I was nothing short of being completely broken.

My gorgeous son, our amazing dog and my wonderful family got me through those dark days and thanks to them life slowly got a little bit easier.

Just eight months into my single life as a working mother, my sister-in-law received a call at work from the secretary of the local, famous and well-respected medium Ronnie Buckingham. He had had a last-minute cancellation that day and would she like to have a reading! We managed to cover her absence so encouraged her to go. She came back to work a few hours later very emotional, but amazed at what he'd said. She said that I'd come through in her reading and that he'd encouraged me to move on and not look back. She therefore felt it would be beneficial for me to see him as hers had given her some hope for the future too. So, with this in mind I picked up the phone and dialled!

I made the call to Ronnie's secretary feeling a mixture of nerves and excitement. I'd heard such amazing things about Ronnie and the joy, peace of mind and reassurance he'd brought to many people. I'd been very fortunate at that time not to have lost many friends or family but the one that I had lost, my step-nan, she was very special to me, and I hoped with all my heart that she'd come through and give me some sort of assurance that one day life would be better.

On arrival Ronnie was friendly and welcoming. He gave me a big smile that quickly eased my nerves and explained what to expect from the session. He popped the tape in the tape recorder and began. Coming back to the here and now I'm very sad to say that I've never been able to find that recording. I've searched for years for it, having known that I would have put it in a very safe place, but it's clearly proved to be too safe! I've ransacked the obvious places! Three house moves since then may have been the cause. I like to think it'll turn up one day in a place I least expect it to be. You never know, a loved one up in the skies may help me with that one day too I hope!

So, all of what I'm retelling here now is from the depths of my memory, however, it had such a profound impact on me at the time that it's etched in my brain forever. Ronnie quickly knew I'd been through very hard and emotional times and explained that he wasn't a fortune teller but would do what he could to shed some light on what my future looked like. He then went on to say that someone named Kath or Katherine was coming through but it was a definite K name. My heart could have burst in that moment as my hopes of my step Nan Kath coming through had come true! He shared many things that confirmed it was her, such as our early morning card and board games that we played together, as well as the laughter she had over our late dog's quirky ways and her constant snoring! They had a love/hate relationship which was so endearing to us all.

Ronnie then moved on to what I was waiting for, a glimpse into my future. I longed to hear that I would meet someone wonderful very soon, that I'd be whisked off my feet and we'd live happily ever after. Sadly, that wasn't the case! Instead, he said that I would meet a few guys over the next few years but that none of them would be right for me and that I'd know that deep down.

His actual words which I remember so clearly were, "You're going to kiss a lot of frogs before the right man comes along!" I had already made a strict pact with myself that a man had to bring nothing but value to my life in order for me to contemplate a future with him. I'd also told myself, that should he ever bring upset or drama into our little world he would be gone in an instant!

Pretty harsh some would say but, in my eyes, life with a man bringing me anguish was a million times worse than me living in my safe little bubble of me, my boy and our dog! Although this was sad to hear I wasn't surprised as my faith in men had completely gone out the window at that point!

But all was not lost. He said that in around 8-10 years' time (gulp!!!), I would meet a man that would take on my son like his own. Cue music to my ears!! He said that he would have been a friend first and that his name was shortened ie Matt instead of Matthew, Dan instead of Daniel or Sam instead of Samuel. I had friends with all of those names at the time but none of them I could see a future with. Ronnie continued that we would be very happy, marry and one day have our own baby boy. I was utterly thrilled to hear that there was hope for me yet. From that day onwards my sparkle returned. It gave me the hope that I so badly craved, and I truly believe that his reading helped me turn that corner.

I felt positive once again and excited for the future. Fast forward a few years and Ronnie was right! I did kiss some frogs and had a couple of relationships that didn't last very long at all. I then had a long spell of not looking anymore as the internet dating world was nothing but a disaster and just not for me. Roll on another five years to 2019 when I happened to notice a post on Facebook from an old friend who I'd always had a soft spot for.

It was a picture of him and his young daughter moving into their new home. 'Here's to a fresh start' it said. After a quick stalk of his Facebook page, I guessed he must have split from his wife. I was with

Clare with Dan - the most incredible stepdad to my son and amazing partner

a girlfriend of mine that afternoon and after me sharing my fond memories of him, she urged me profusely to message him. It didn't take much convincing and much to my delight he instantly replied! For the first time in what felt like forever I had a feeling of sheer elation and happiness. We quickly arranged a date for a week's time. I'm delighted to say the rest is history!

His name is Dan, and he is the most incredible stepdad to my son and amazing partner. Again, Ronnie was right!

A couple of months into our relationship, I got to meet the entire family at Dan's brother's birthday get together in a pub in Braintree. I walked in and was absolutely astounded to see Ronnie Buckingham sitting at the table in front of me. I could see Dan's mum near to him so assumed he was her friend. Dan then introduced me to him as 'Ronnie, my brother-in-law!!'. My jaw nearly hit the floor! I couldn't believe it! Despite being super friendly I could tell he didn't recognise me, so I refrained from blurting out that I'd seen him all those years ago and that everything he'd told me had come true!!

Since then, I have been welcomed with open arms into the Jones's family and I feel truly blessed to be a part of them. Ronnie and I have a lovely relationship and I thank him from the bottom of my heart for giving me that hope and strength I so desperately needed at that time. I can honestly say I'm the happiest I have ever been, and I'm thrilled to say that Dan proposed to me on Christmas Eve 2020 at home with our children. We are getting married in the South of France at a beautiful Chateau this coming August where 45 of our family and friends will be joining us for the weekend. What's even more amazing is that Ronnie will be marrying us!

The man that predicted our happiness all those years ago will be sealing the deal in his very own words. We couldn't think of anyone more perfect to do it.

With every success story comes a little sadness though and ours has been losing our baby in November 2023. With me working with children, and Dan being such an amazing father and children adoring him everywhere we go, it was a no brainer for us that although older than the average parents, we wanted one of our own to complete our little family. We were thrilled to fall pregnant in October 2022, but sadly had our first miscarriage seven weeks later. It was a devastating loss to us both but together we stood strong and our love for each other got us through.

We tried again and were elated to find out that we'd fallen again in August 2023. We were petrified of losing again so had some early scans and all seemed well. However, it was at our dating scan at 13 weeks that they found that our baby had Patau Syndrome. Of course, this news came as a huge blow. They informed us that if we were to have our baby, he/she would have only hours, maybe a few days to live.

To also hear that it's only a one in four thousand chance of this happening to a couple was devastating. Those next few weeks were horrendous and seemed to go by in a blur. I had to give birth to our baby at 15 weeks. However, I found huge comfort in being able to say our goodbyes in the privacy of the bereavement suite at the hospital. He was a beautiful baby boy and we named him Devon. He will be forever etched in our hearts and a day doesn't go by without us thinking of him and what could have been.

Dan and I are so grateful for what we have though and maybe one day we will have our boy that Ronnie predicted, but if we don't that's ok too. Devon was enough, and always will be.

Clare

Hi my name is Kerry Chadwick and this is from my Facebook post back on the 16th August 2017

Kerry with her nan

Sooo... tonight we went to see Ronnie Buckingham in Elmstead Market. A couple of months ago, I lost my dear nan's ring that she gave me before she passed.

I'm devastated, as I'm usually so careful. I have been so annoyed at myself.

Earlier today while I was in the car alone, I asked my nan out loud to tell me tonight where the ring was.

So tonight, firstly my dear brother came through. Ronnie got every detail right of his passing. Even came out with his name! and said some other bits that were absolutely spot on. Then went on to say that my grandad was there with him, and Ronnie described him to a 'T' too.

And then finally my dear nan was there... telling me where my ring was!! Ronnie described the ring and then told me it was in a laundry basket or with clothes. So, when we got in, we looked again and we found it in a basket in my bedroom that I'd had some clothes on top of.

Thank you so much Ronnie Buckingham. I'm so pleased I have my nan's ring back and am so happy to hear from my brother, grandad and nan!

Many thanks Kerry

CQMS Stanley Savill (3244621)

As part of the 7th (Light Infantry) Parachute Battalion my grandfather CQMS Stanley Savill (3244621) fought in the DD Campaign of June 1944 that would finally break the Nazi stranglehold on mainland Europe

His battalion's task was to parachute into

enemy occupied territory in advance of the main landing brigade, capture the Pegasus and Orne Bridges, and defend them until the main assault brigade arrived.

That he and his colleagues achieved this successfully in difficult conditions and hostile terrain was one of the war's defining moments and testament to the heroism of the men.

Sadly, only eight days later, whilst preparing a hot meal for his men, a mortar attack rained down on their position. CQMS Savill was killed at the tender age of 28.

Only through stories passed down by my mother and grandmother have I got to know him so when Ronnie invited me in for a private reading on the 28th of February 2023, I responded with nervous expectation. "Will he come through?", "Will he know who I am?".

Well, I got all of that and more. From the reading it was clear that Stan, wherever he is, was well versed in our families' lives and Ronnie was the perfect medium through which to converse.

The number of intricate details Stan conveyed through Ronnie could not be made up. For example, he knew I had a daughter, he knew she went to university in the north, and he found it humorous that she has recently taken possession of a giant toy panda! All true!!

I got teary eyed though when Ronnie explained that I nearly died on the operating table when I was 19 during a lung operation. It seems granddad knew it wasn't my time and helped push me back, Ronnie assuring me that I would be around for a while yet!

I got more goosebumps when I was given a personal message from my granddad, Ronnie telling me that what was gnawing away at me in life was the fact that I overthink everything. How can he know what I'm thinking I thought as I stood to shake Ronnie's hand with a tranquil sense of relief and peace descending over me and a determination to live life to the fullest as a result.

Steve George

CHAPTER 12

INSIDE THE CAGE

In this chapter we look at an Essex landmark which is called The Cage and delve further into its sinister history:

The day Steph visited The Cage in St Osyth to research it further for this book, the skies above were a slate grey and looking rather ominous. The house which stands in the middle of this Essex village,

once a sunshine yellow, now looks

abandoned with paint peeling from the cobwebbed window frames. To the right of the property is a dark, leafy path referred to by locals as 'Coffin Walk'. It's supposed to be where the bodies of those women who had not survived their incarceration inside the Cage, were secretly spirited away by stretcher in the dead of night up to the village graveyard. *The Cage is so called as it was once a prison for witches, and a place where local criminals would be kept. As you step inside the thick, ancient oak door into what is now the living room, beneath you, now nailed down for good reason, is a threatening pit. This is where women like Ursula Kemp were unceremoniously flung to await their trial. Some didn't even survive to reach their trial. Those that did were either hanged, drowned or burnt to death, often in front of the other villagers. It was a barbaric time in our English history. So-called witchcraft was feared by many, and witch hunts were aplenty. Between the 16th and 18th centuries Britain was awash with witch trials, led by the notorious Matthew Hopkins, a self-appointed Witchfinder General, who held court between 1644 and 1647. Hopkins (c.1620-1647) lived in Mistley, less than 30 minutes ride from St Osyth. His very first accusation being in neighbouring Manningtree.

Plaque on the exterior wall of the Cage in St Osyth

As many as 300 people were executed for witchcraft in eastern England during this period. In nearby Chelmsford

19 were hanged for witchcraft in one day, which included two from St Osyth.

It wasn't until almost a century later that the laws against witchcraft were repealed in 1736.

The Cage was used as a medieval prison and 14 supposed local witches were held in the pit inside in 1582 to await their fate.

Original heavy oak door leading into The Cage

These unfortunate women, known as the 'Witches of St Osyth', were sent to trial. Of the 14, eight were found guilty and they were sentenced to death by hanging on the gallows. Ursula Kemp was one of those poor, helpless women alongside Elizabeth Bennett. Women who were at the mercy of the other villagers.

Ursula had been a midwife in St Osyth. She was well liked and also helped where she could, tending to the sick and needy in the village. After a feud with another local family, rumours of her methods of healing began to circulate and she was accused of witchcraft. Nowadays we pour scorn on those who create a so-called witch-hunt, i.e. accusing someone without any facts. Now you can see exactly where the term derives from.

It all stemmed from a fellow neighbour of Ursulas accusing her of healing a sick child by chanting incantations – magic spells and using charms. The rumours grew and soon she was also accused of death by bewitchment. Gossip was rife with tales that she had killed a local person by using her incantations.

Her trial was based around the testimony of an eight-year-old boy from the town, who testified she had confessed to using witchcraft. As ridiculous as it seems the court ruled against Ursula, and she was found guilty and was hanged for her 'crimes.'

At some point during the 1800s, The Cage, which was little more than a shed with an oak door and a pit, was rebuilt using bricks and mortar. It continued to be used as a jail until 1908, holding local delinquents and drunks before they stood trial. Certainly, by the 1970s, The Cage had been transformed into a house. A developer with imagination turning the former medieval prison into a living room and adding bedrooms upstairs. It was in 2005 that Vanessa Mitchell purchased The Cage as a home.

The Cage transformed into a home

*Source: St Osyth Museum

Vanessa recalls, "I remembered seeing the plaque outside, but I don't remember being scared of it. I'd lived in St

Osyth as a child and so my earliest memories were of just being fascinated by the house. I suppose you could say I was drawn to it. "Once move in day was over things soon took a more sinister turn.

Vanessa who had owned the Cage in St Osyth since 2004 explains, "I saw apparitions walk through my room and would hear ghostly growls." She was pushed over by spirits whilst pregnant and even spanked on the bottom by a ghost! She regularly saw objects fly around the kitchen. During her time living at The Cage Vanessa was also punched, bitten, and thrown to the floor. Mysterious figures would appear to float through her home and even attack her guests.

Vanessa invited the local vicar at one point to come and bless The Cage. As he took out his Holy Water he told her, "I've been in lots of parishes, but never since I've come to the parish of St Osyth, have I had so many people coming to me in private, and coming to me in church, saying "I need you to come to bless the house, I've got a haunted house." I can tell you of at least four houses up this road I've been into."

The blessing sadly had no effect and the activity continued. At one point during her time at The Cage, Vanessa explained she could hear voices telling her to end her own life. A previous owner of the property had done exactly that by hanging, according to local documents.

Eventually it became too much. After three years of poltergeist activity, Vanessa moved out, fearing for her young son's safety, following the constant activity from the spirits and feelings of being forced out. After moving out to a friend's house, she let the property out to another friend, only for them to leave just four months later. Next it was let out to a young couple with a child, who abandoned the house within two months of moving in.

However, her experiences have been documented in a book, *Spirits of the Cage: True Accounts of Living in a Haunted Medieval Prison* by Richard Estep. There is also going to be a film made entitled *The Cage*. which will further tell the story of Vanessa's haunted years.

The property was put up for sale for £180,000 in February 2016 and in 2019 an offer was made by another woman to buy The Cage described as a 'two-bedroom cottage' for around £240,000. Since the sale, the new owner has never lived in the property, and it is once again up for sale by local agents.

Back in August 2020 Vanessa invited Medium Ronnie Buckingham, to conduct a reading inside the living room at The Cage. The following is a direct transcript from his reading caught on video from that day. The picture (left) shows Ronnie sitting in a wing-backed leather armchair as he begins to tune into the spirit world.

Ronnie begins, "There's a real mix of some not very nice and some angry, but also some innocent spirits here in this house.

There's such a mixture here. My first overwhelming thought is that a lot of these spirits are tired.

They are tired of being investigated. They are tired of being looked at. It's almost like they want to rest but haven't been allowed to. I get the feeling that some of them can't find their way back. Or through things that happened to them, in this property, they felt restricted to it, and they are angry.

The first person I feel coming through is a very pretty, blonde-haired little boy. Only a little tot, probably four or five? He's wearing a sailor's outfit so maybe Victorian times, late 1800s. For some reason I feel that he passed before that. I feel like he's wearing the outfit to show me that his dad was at sea. His dad was a sailor. I feel his dad was permanently away at sea and that the mother figure passed around about 37 – 40s. I get the name of her as being something like Mary or Mary Anne might even be a Maryanne. The little boy is either Jacob or Jake. He's got lots of pus and boils so that takes him back to maybe being a plague victim. He's a lovely, harmless little fella. Anything that moves on the floor around here will be due to him because he plays. He's not unhappy, he's just stuck in this time warp.

I feel that this house has lots of things going on from lots of different generations. Some of these spirits aren't aware of other spirits in the house. Now there's also a lady coming through who fell to her death here. She broke her neck. I feel the name Anne connects to her in some way, could be it's her middle name. Could be Annie. She would be later than the little boy and I feel it was only 100 years or so ago. I feel that she was found at the foot of the stairs.

When I look beyond her, I feel there's another lady who was accused of something that she wasn't. I don't believe this woman ever was a witch. I think she either had the gift like me or healed and for that she was incarcerated. She's telling me that what really did it for her and why she's so angry is that the goaler [the jailer] or the magistrate whoever he was, also used her for sex. On the pretense that he could get her out of trouble by putting a word in for her. I feel this woman wasn't a young woman perhaps in her 40s? Quite attractive, quite chesty. I feel that he had sex with her on more than one occasion. This woman's annoyance was for not only being tried for something that she didn't do but also that she let him do sexual things to her and he never kept his word."

Podcaster Freddie with Ronnie and Vanessa

The video was shot as part of a podcast series, of which

Vanessa is one of the hosts - The Haunted Podcast. Her friend Freddie is one of the producers and fellow presenters. Ronnie starts to pick up on Freddie's Grandfather who brought him up.

He says, "I feel like I've got a much older man here, but he feels like a father to you. Would he have been connected in some way to this house?" Freddie's Grandfather lived just a few doors away from The Cage on the same street.

Ronnie continues, "He worked with his hands like a builder." Freddie confirms that his grandfather used to work on the roads. Ronnie says, "There was no chance to say goodbye he's telling me." Freddie confirms this. Ronnie goes on to say, "He's showing me a pen knife. So not sure if someone in your family now owns that pen knife? Freddie confirms that this is also correct.

Ronnie goes back to the spirits in The Cage, "I do know that two people have committed suicide in this house. One definitely by hanging, a man." Vanessa confirms this saying, "Yes, it was a few years before I moved in. He hung himself from the beam above the stairs." Ronnie says, "Also a woman who cut her wrists something like with a broken window she was someone who was accused of witchcraft and she didn't want to face the gallows or the fire. I'm not sure if that killed her but she tried to take her own life. She's got baskets full of poppies, but they are not the flowers but the poppy heads. Not sure if she was a herbalist or made some sort of opium and I can smell pipe smoke with her as she comes through."

In April 2024, as part of the research into this new book, we approached Vanessa Mitchell to ask about that unique reading she witnessed in the living room of her former home with Ronnie Buckingham, four years earlier. Here is our exclusive interview with Vanessa, from her new home, also an old cottage just round the corner from The Cage.

The lady bought it [The Cage] and has never moved into it. She does believe in ghosts, but she didn't think it was anything to worry about. She would make light of it. She's a lovely lady and I met her son once. He didn't want her to buy the house, but she did it anyway.

Vanessa now lives in another traditional cottage, steeped in history, which is over 500 years old. As we sit chatting in her living room, opposite the glow from the log burner I see on one of the ancient beams there is a plaque which reads Beware of the Ghosts.

It's a world away from where she lived before. The Cage where she lived with her young son. Vanessa continues ….

Ronnie with Vanessa inside The Cage, her former home

Initially I'd known Ronnie for years when he used to be a bouncer in Colchester, and we've had similar friends over the years. I remember back then hearing that he'd gone from being a bouncer to being a Medium and I was like I couldn't believe it! I was like, "Stop It!!" Ronnie always had a fierce reputation on the doors.

Nobody was going to ever mess with Ronnie! I got in contact with him again after years as I do a podcast with Freddie. It's about paranormal stuff. We wanted Ronnie on there, so we decided to bring Ronnie to The Cage to do the interview. I've still got the video of the moment he did the reading. [Transcribed above.]

Ronnie is a really straight fella, there's no bullshit with him. Sometimes I think he tells too much! I know that he would much rather say 'I can't pick up a bloody thing!' than lie about it.

I think Ronnie is a fantastic Medium. He's incredible. He told me something that hardly anybody in my family knew. I remember I was just talking to him on the phone standing in my garden. It's something that I never even knew till years ago. At that moment I thought this fella is the real deal. So, I've got huge respect for him. I believe Ronnie is definitely up there as one of the top Mediums in the country. His ability to talk to the dead, he's absolutely incredible. I've met literally loads and loads of Mediums in the past since having The Cage. I can say that Ronnie is definitely the real deal.

Ronnie is good at detail. I can't share with you the one major thing he told me that day over the phone, as it's something private which is why I was so shocked when he came right out and said it. If my own family don't know it, how the hell does Ronnie know it? Unless he was speaking to the person who was involved. [who has since passed] *You couldn't guess it; you couldn't make it up.*

Our grateful thanks to Vanessa Mitchell, for her help in contributing to this chapter. To listen to her podcast check out @thehauntedpodcastofficial

CHAPTER 13

NO TIME TO SAY GOODBYE

I always say there are no goodbyes. In France they say À bientôt! which means see you soon.

I'd like to start this chapter by talking a little bit about Suicide. Some people think that if you take your own life then you will go to Hell. That's not the case at all. Yes, an evil person would go to a darker place. Adolf Hitler supposedly took his own life so he would be a candidate for the darker realms. However, a nice person who has got depression or perhaps can't stand the thought of dying a painful death of cancer, they pass over like the rest of your loved ones to a better place.

I also get my fair share of suicides. One was a young man that had hanged himself and another that had taken an overdose. I try to explain that there isn't actually a hell. In this world here on earth you can be a horrible soul in amongst nice people. Over there you don't get that chance. Hell is devoid of any colour, its cold, its purgatory really. Bereft of love or any animals so it is a kind of hell in that sense. If you get someone who takes their own life, for example the singer George Michael.

You have to also look at all the good he did whilst he was on this earth. Without telling anyone, he donated millions of pounds to charities so he wouldn't have gone to hell.

I think that people who are terminally ill and take their own life, yes they may have to come back and pay their time again here on earth, but they don't go to a dark place either. I remember another man who came through to me. He was in loads of debt; he was going to lose the house and he took his own life so that the family didn't have to be put on the streets. I just want to tell you that there isn't this straightforward Heaven/Hell situation over there. Only a nasty piece of work would end up down there. Here's Lynda's testimonial …

Ronnie, we came to one of your workshops just a few weeks after losing my son, obviously you did not know this, during the day you stopped what you were doing and said, "Has someone here just lost a son to suicide?" Nobody answered you. I thought he can't be talking to me surely? You said "His name is Shane, Shaun or similar" I realised then that yes you were talking to us. I was there with his partner Julie, obviously we cried, it was so raw. You asked who George is. I told you that his son is George. You went on "Is he on the other side too?" Then I realised that you knew Shaun was with his old school friend George. He lays next to him in the churchyard, as sadly a few months before Shaun died, George was murdered.

Shaun told you about his partner's previously volatile marriage. You said that Shaun was telling you that his partner Julie had tidied him up in the chapel of rest, which she did.

You said that his sister had touched his feet, which she also did. Shaun also told you that Julie goes to his grave too much.

You asked who Glen or Glynis was, you said, "She's crazy and singing I'm getting married in the morning!" My sister Glenda passed many years ago, a short time before her death she was singing this song, and miming sewing. When I asked her what she was up to she said, "I am finishing Noo's (her daughter Nikki) wedding dress."

You asked about Nobby or Del, my dad was Derek Clark. You described a little pearlised apple knife that he had given to Shaun. I had completely forgotten about this. You said the knife would be in Shaun's things somewhere. You told me it might be a while before I find it as he lived in Australia for many years and a lot of his things are still there with a friend.

You told me about Shaun's children and that one of them has special needs. Talking to you was a great help and very unexpected, obviously the pain is very raw as this was only three months ago.

Keep up the good work

Lynda X

There are always lots of complex reasons why people sadly resort to taking their own life.

Only the other night I did a reading to a group in Hertfordshire near Enfield. In the group there was a lady and her son came through to me. I was able to tell her that he was electrocuted on the train tracks. He fell asleep on the train after a few drinks on a night out with his friends.

I could see them larking about and laughing as they left him on the train asleep. He woke and he tried to leave the train across the tracks alone a few stops further on. It wasn't suicide, he simply fell onto the tracks.

Instead of going over the bridge because he'd had a drink he fell over and onto the line. She was amazed at the detail I was able to bring her.

My past is out there, for all to read about. As you know I was a bad boy in the past but it's quite interesting that I do seem to attract past villains who have passed over. I remember an old cockney lady came to see me. She had been looking for many years for someone to come through to her. It was her brother and I got him and named him. He used to be nicknamed the Mad Axeman, Frankie Mitchell. I was able to tell her he was with me and she was absolutely over the moon. She's probably passed over herself now as I remember she told me that she'd hung on to life after life because she wanted to know the truth about what had happened to her brother. He was murdered, she knew that but not how. I was able to tell her that he was weighted down and his body had been dropped in the sea and that was where he was. She left my home happy on that day.

Another time a young girl came for a reading and it was either her granddad or great granddad who came through. When I say young girl, she was probably in her 30s. I knew that he'd been shot in East London in a pub there. It turned out it was George Cornell who was shot by one of the Kray Twins.

[On 9 March 1966, Ronnie Kray shot and murdered George Cornell, an associate of a rival gang, the Richardsons, as he was sitting at the bar. The murder took place in the then saloon bar.]

I was back at Marconatos in Hoddeston just the other night and another professional boxer Billy Morgan was there in the audience along with his mate and they were joking with me before I began. They told me that they were purely there for the girls that night. By the end of that evening, I had them both absolutely sobbing their hearts out when their family came through. Here's Billy's testimonial from that night …

I'm not too sure what to say or how to say it, but the night we attended Ronnie's night at Marconatos, I wasn't even aware of the type of night we were attending. I was told by my partner Lauren we were going out for the night with our friends Amy and Billy.

I had a bit of a nightmare on the day we went to see Ronnie. I had a rubbish day on the golf course full of wind and rain, and then on the way home my back tyre blew out on the M25.

When I was in the car on the way to Hoddesdon, myself and Billy were so sceptical about the night. I have seen mediums in the past, the first time I saw a medium I left in tears. The next time I see the same medium I realised it was a script they followed and I left so disappointed. I have always said if a medium can give me names or events then I would believe in the medium. Ronnie did both.

Not only did Ronnie mention names, my dad's cousins names, his best mates names, my sons, where I'm from, and even what sport I did. He described my dad to a tee. A few things Ronnie said didn't make sense but after speaking to my mum it all made sense. Hand on heart, my heart was pumping through my chest, I was in tears.
I had people coming up to me at the end of the night asking if it was all true. It was such an unbelievable experience I struggle to put the emotions into words.

Thanks Billy Morgan

Billy's mate, also called Billy, who is a Scaffolder has also kindly given me a testimonial of his take on that same night. You can read it in Chapter 11.

Me with Rae Edwina Brown, Spiritualist Artist and Medium alongside boxer Gary Mason

Another time I recall I was at a charity event, which was hosted by Paul Ross. The British Professional Boxer Gary Mason was there that night.

Also present on that evening was Dave Courteney, a well-known gangster. I gave him a message from his Dad. His dad told me something that had happened to them in Tenerife. I was a bit apprehensive telling Dave in case he cut up funny with me. However, afterwards he was as good as gold. He came over to me and shook my hand saying, "Mate what you told me, that thing in Tenerife. No one knows about that." He had a mate with him, and I got his daughter coming through.

As I mentioned earlier in Chapter 1, restaurants can reach those people who wouldn't go to a spiritualist church.

Even the biggest sceptic, especially the men will go to a restaurant. They think I'll have a drink and at least I'll get a nice meal beforehand. I always make sure that I have a laugh with them to put them at their ease. Interestingly though, by doing the restaurants I've converted so many non-believers in the afterlife. It's the weird stuff that comes through which makes them truly believe without a shadow of a doubt. The other day I got a man came through to me. I said to the audience, "You'll know if it's your dad I have here with me as he's doing tricks with yoyos." It turned out he was a British Champion YoYo person in his day. How random is that?!

I got a message from Paramount years ago saying that they were thinking of doing a new DVD release of the film Ghost. They were going to release the DVD again with another DVD talking to Patrick Swayze and Whoopie Goldberg about some of the weird things that had happened on set during the making of the film Ghost. So, the film company contacted me, saying will you come to London as we are promoting this new release on 17 different radio stations all around the country. First Radio

Liverpool comes on and introduces me and asks me about the film Ghost and then asks me to tell them something about the presenter. I can honestly say, out of the 17 radio station presenters I spoke to that day, I absolutely nailed 16 of them. The 17th well he wouldn't have any of it. The people from Paramount were delighted with me, saying if we ever do something like that again, we will definitely be giving you a call.

I have also read the son of Charlie Richardson although he was never acknowledged by his father. However, he has done his DNA testing and traced it back. His mum had a fling with Charlie and this chap is the result of that. The Richardsons were a rival gang who ruled South London with the Krays ruling East London.

Whilst still on this side of life, I once met Tony Tucker at the Pitsea Carriage Company car dealers owned by Roger Pike in Pitsea in Essex. Years later he was one of the three killed in the Rettendon Range Rover murders* After his death, Tony also came through to me once in a private reading I was doing for one of his girlfriends from his past. Then he came through to me again to a member of his family, during a show that I was doing.

Before you ask, I'm not going to say that he told me who killed him, or who the murderer was. I can say that it definitely wasn't the men who are in prison for it.

* Patrick Tate, Anthony Tucker and Craig Rolfe were all found shot dead in a Range Rover near the isolated farm track at Rettendon, Essex in December 1995 All three had been shot in the head, while

Tate was also blasted in the stomach - an act which some have speculated was to silence him while his friends in the front were executed. The bodies of the three men were found the following morning by farmer Peter and his friend Ken Jiggins as they went to feed the farm's 800 pheasants. Jack Whomes and Michael Steele were convicted of the murders in January 1998 and sentenced to life imprisonment, despite protesting their innocence. Whomes has since been released. *Source: National press

I've often wondered why I can bring these types of people through in particular? Maybe it's because I can speak their language I really don't know, but I do find it interesting.

*I've had my fair share of murders to talk about as part of past readings. A lady came to me, she was quite a regular of mine. On this occasion she came with another woman and when I opened the door, she said to me, "I'm really sorry Ronnie, but could this lady have the reading instead of me?" Of course I agreed. I've got to be honest, I held this lady's hand and it really made me feel ill. I told her, "I've got a young woman coming through here and I believe it's your daughter."

I told her I could see lots and lots of blood. I said, "Oh she was murdered!" I could see in my mind a hammer so I asked if she was killed with a hammer and the lady confirmed that she was. I said that she had two children and that she was no longer with their father. I knew that she had a boy and a girl. She gave nothing away to me and I suddenly said, "Oh my God they are also with her! They were also murdered on the same night!!'

I said it wasn't by their dad, it was by a lover who was also a drug addict." I told her that he was like the Devil incarnate. I said he was Irish and that his name was actually Damien. Then I said, "With your children, why do I see another little girl with, what I can only describe as, Chinese looking eyes? I feel she also passed over with them?" It turned out that the daughter had had a friend to come over for a sleepover.

This happened in the North of England somewhere maybe like Sheffield? This lady had come from the North for a reading as so far, she'd been disappointed with other mediums she'd had read for her. This was, I think, about two years ago. The only bit I didn't get was that he also raped her 11-year-old daughter before he killed her. The killer tied the mum up, raped the daughter then with a hammer he killed her son, then her daughter and killed her little friend who was staying over. I told her that this happened on a Saturday.

I said the friend had stayed over on the Friday and was meant to go home the next morning. She'd had such a nice time on the Friday that she called her mum and asked if she could stay over for one more night.

The lady told me after the reading that the killer actually went outside the house, stood in the front garden and phoned the police. He told the police, "I'm going back to prison as I've just killed four people."

As far as I know they've only just demolished the house. Very rarely do I ever cry but I got them out of the door that day and I broke down. I phoned my Nicky up and I was sobbing, it hurt me to do the reading. This poor woman had lost her daughter who was her only child, her grandson and her granddaughter and her granddaughter's little friend. It's heartbreaking what you see and what you feel. I got such a lovely text back from the lady's friend afterwards. She put in her text that she thought I'd saved this woman's sanity, it was such a good reading. It has given her some hope that her family are all still there somewhere.

[*In September 2021 Terri Harris, 35, and John Paul, 13, and Lacey Bennett, 11, were killed along with Connie Gent, 11. At Derby crown court Damien Bendall, 32, admitted murdering his partner, Terri Harris, 35, and her two children from a previous relationship – John Paul Bennett, 13, and Lacey Bennett, 11 – as well as Lacey's friend Connie Gent, 11. He also admitted raping Lacey.

The victims' bodies were discovered at the family home in Killamarsh, Derbyshire, on 19 September, where Bendall was staying at the time. Mr Justice Sweeney sentenced Bendall to five whole-life sentences, one for each murder and the rape, meaning he will never be released from prison.] *Source: National press December 2022.

My story of Ronnie Buckingham is when I went to one of his shows for the first time around 18 months ago in Braintree. I went there with my cousin who had lost his father. I had never been before. He started to describe a man that had sadly been taken from us in a horrific way. Ronnie described him as very tall, stocky and with dark hair. He mentioned about him also having a son. I knew then it was my uncle Marcus that came through to him.

He was sadly taken from us after being stabbed by his girlfriend over drug money. It was lovely to hear how proud of us he was and that he was so proud to see that my cousin had become a dad himself. This message from Marcus has had a huge impact on both me and my cousin. My cousin more so, as he hadn't seen his dad in around a year prior to his death, as his mum had moved up north with him.

It was really lovely to hear from him through Ronnie and to witness that connection Ronnie has with the other side.

Thank you so much for your message that day Ronnie.

Lesley Chipperfield

Five years ago, my 19-year-old son, James, set off for an evening out with his friends with a "see you later mum" as he walked out of the door. Later never came, James never came home. He died in a tragic accident. The police woke me in the early hours with this devastating news. Every parent's absolute worst nightmare.

A few weeks later, after the funeral, one of my friends told me about Ronnie. She had been to one of his evening events after her father died and was blown away when Ronnie passed on a message to her from her dad.

I had never ever given mediums a second thought, I had no cause to. But when your world implodes after the person you created, carried, gave birth to, loved and nurtured, dies randomly unexpectedly and suddenly out of the blue, I found that I now desperately needed proof of life after death.

It was less than seven weeks after my son died that my husband drove me to see Ronnie one evening. We turned up, paid at the door and nervously took our seats, not knowing what to expect. My son was the third message that evening. Being so early on in my grief, still in shock and feeling numb, I could barely believe what Ronnie was saying. I was confused and sobbing. Ronnie was giving me information that he could only be getting from my son. He described James to us, and he talked about the circumstances around his death. Ronnie told me what football team he supported, gave me family names and dates etc. It was astonishing. I was literally flabbergasted.

I spoke to Ronnie at the end of the evening and thanked him so much for my message. I was so very grateful.

My friend suggested I try to get a private reading with Ronnie and I've been lucky to have had two private readings with Ronnie during that first year (before COVID hit).

I was sure he was speaking with my son James.

In my first private reading, Ronnie provided me with so much detailed information that I was sure he was speaking with my son. Together with all this detail, Ronnie told me three things in particular that only my son would know. Evidence!

My husband sat in on the reading with me and Ronnie connected him with his father also. I left Ronnie's that day feeling lifted, comforted and less anguished.

By the time I had my second private reading, my mother and my son's dad (my ex-husband) had died. Ronnie didn't know, of course, but they came through with my son. I was again blown away with all the details Ronnie gave me, two things which particularly provided absolute evidence that they live on. One being my mother's name (not a common name). You can't guess a name! Ronnie was connecting with my mother and my son and my ex-husband. It was so truly emotional and comforting to know they live on. Again, I felt less anguished that day after seeing Ronnie.

Over the past four years I have travelled to see Ronnie five times at his evening events and have been so fortunate to have received a message from my son at four of those evenings. I'm so very grateful. It keeps me going.

Ronnie, my son clearly really likes you! Thank you so much for all you do, for giving us hope and providing comfort and helping to heal our broken hearts a little, with confirmation that life goes on after death. I always remember you told me Ronnie - your son is still alive, he's just in another room. One day I'll be able to walk into that room and hug him for all eternity, but until then I'll keep holding on. Getting through each day, hoping that my son comes to say hello sometimes at Ronnie's evening events.

Thank you so very, very much Ronnie, what a wonderful gift you have.

James' mum, Carol

Our Story

Life is for living, but sometimes it's very hard. I returned from working in the Middle East early 2013 as my mother had been diagnosed with

December 2010 Left to right William, Dad, Louis & Mum.

Pancreatic Cancer and sadly, we lost her June 2013. At the time, losing my mother hit me hard, but little did I know this was only the start.

I then lost my eldest Son, Louis in 2014 in the space of 24 hours to DKA (Diabetic ketoacidosis). The care he received from both the NHS and then Great Ormond Street was phenomenal, but sadly he left us so traumatically.

Losing Louis was horrific and to be honest it is true what they say, as a parent, losing a child is your worst nightmare. Working through this, I then lost my father in 2018, a huge character and another empty space. As we worked through this Heidi my wife lost her grandma, who was a role model for her, and the grieving process started again. We know Ronnie from the local gym and always stopped to say hello and have a chat, a lovely guy and occasionally he would say "I see you have your mate with you".

Heidi knows Ronnie's background and is very much a believer. I, on the other hand whilst believing there is something in the afterlife, verged on the sceptical side. In 2022 we decided to arrange a private reading for both of us, which we both loved; however Dad came through so strongly, which is not a surprise as he was such a huge character. So, we decided to book separate private readings, which were so different. Ronnie makes you feel comfortable and relaxed and then he starts. All of a sudden, it's like your lost loved ones are in the room.

The whole experience left us in no doubt there is an afterlife and we both came away feeling at peace. For me, I just wanted to hear that Louis was ok, strange I know. The conversations we all had left us in no doubt Ronnie has a gift and it was an experience we shall never forget. If we needed further proof of this gift, Louis, through Ronnie, said that he could see the Actors Equity mask for William, my youngest son. Following auditions, he has recently been accepted into the Italia Conti Drama School to continue his journey and follow his dream of being in the West End.

Mark, William and Heidi.

When I listen to my reading, I still get a sense of peace together with a feeling that life does go on, we just can't see it and it makes me smile.

Mark & Heidi Hackett 2024.

I was working on a door in Great Yarmouth, Sue was a waitress in a hotel. I walked past and said 'I'm gonna marry her!'. That night I saw her in a disco, asked her for a dance, and one week later I asked her to marry me. We loved each other instantly and were married within a year, June 5th 1976. She gave me a life men can only dream of, she was perfect.

Together for 42 incredible years, and then suddenly from out of the blue — boom! Tragedy struck. Sue was diagnosed with the same type of leukemia that I have, but a vicious and aggressive form. She put up one hell of a fight and not once did she ever complain— my warrior fairy princess!! But on April 27th 2018 at 1.27am she blew us two kisses and slipped away.

We loved each other instantly

Sometime after losing Sue, our three beautiful children, Danielle, Lisa and Ben got us tickets to see this so-called legend of mediumship, Ronnie Buckingham. I said, "Yeah alright, bollocks!" but was dragged along. During the show I walked out to have a 'Jimmy' 'cos I wasn't that interested, when all of a sudden, they came out running saying, "Dad, Dad, this message is for you".

I went back in and Ronnie was giving a reading. I knew instantly it was my Sue. His accuracy blew my head off!

He knew things he couldn't possibly know about Sue, or me.

He knew things he couldn't possibly know about Sue.

He said 'I have a woman here, very beautiful and kind. He knew she had died from an aggressive blood cancer, that we met in Great Yarmouth and we were soul mates. That the love between us was unbelievably strong.

He said that I wear her rings around my neck, and something else that's very personal to her. They were hidden under my jumper but I wear Sue's rings and her silver angel wings on a necklace.

He knew she was an East End girl from Bow in London. That I'd just recently laid 13 red roses (I had just been to Great Yarmouth and laid 13 red roses, in each of the places we used to go, where we first kissed, where I proposed, and our old flat etc.).

He knew about my past, that I was a bit of a naughty boy, but that spirit didn't save me, she did. Sue told him things in the reading that couldn't be mentioned in public but were absolutely true.

I've since had a private reading with him, and said, "Fuck off Ronnie you couldn't possibly know all that!", but he does. He replied to me, "It's not me Bob, it's Sue telling me."

I have nothing more than respect and admiration for the man and the work he does, and in the words of the prophet – he is the absolute bollocks.

"It's not me Bob, it's Sue telling me."

Thank you, Ronnie, for making people's burden of grief a little easier to carry. You have got me through some dark times.

Bob Aldridge, Harlow

When I was living in France, I was asked to do a piece for the BBC's Inside Out. They brought me back to the UK from France. I was living over there by this time and the people from Mystic Challenge who I used to regularly work with [see Chapter 11] got in touch. They said they'd recommended me to the BBC.

They told me, you'll be picked up and brought back to the UK to do a reading and so I agreed. I didn't know at the time what it was about. I remember the car took me to Detling in Kent. Cameras were there when I arrived and there was a psychic fair going on.

To be honest I was a bit dubious as there were a range of wannabe Mediums there and stalls selling crystals and all these alternative types. There was a table up on the stage with a couple sat at it. *It was a man and a woman and I was asked if I could do a reading for them. I had a camera shoved right in my face, so I felt quite nervous, but I held the lady's hand and I said, "I feel I have a daughter coming through to you here." The lady confirmed by saying simply, "Yes." I continued, "She's with another woman, an Irish lady called Margaret or Peggy." The lady confirmed that was her daughter's Nan.

I went on to say, "I don't know how she passed [the daughter] but it was very near, and I mean very near to where she lived. I feel like it's almost just beyond the garden." The couple both told me, "Yes."

I told the lady, "You told your mum not to take your daughter to the shops for sweets, you said don't take her there. It was because they had to cross the motorway. What I could see was a dip in the motorway where cars would disappear and then come back into view right on top of you. I could see that the Nan did take the daughter across the road to the sweet shop. She couldn't see anything coming, got halfway across the road and a car appeared out of nowhere and killed them both outright.

Sometimes the spirit world puts an image into my mind of something or someone to add to the message. I said to the couple that day, "I keep seeing an image of Jade Goody." I said, "Does Jade refer to your daughter?" The couple nodded saying that Jade was indeed the name of the daughter who they had lost. Anyway, they were over the moon with that and with the rest of the reading I gave them.

The dad said to me, "Look could you possibly get Jade's nickname. It's something that I always called her, and no one has ever got it. We'd finished the filming by then so we went away and sat together in a quiet corner, so that I could really concentrate. It's how messages come through to me, I said, "I know that it's two words and that they rhyme. One of them is like a title, like King, Queen and he agreed with me saying, "Yes." I said, "As for the second word I'm asking her but I can't quite hear what she's saying, it sounds like she's saying Light, Dark, Light, Dark, it's almost like I'm in the shade. Then I said, "Shady Lady." That was it, that was the nickname he always called his daughter, Jade.

*In 2000, eight-year-old Jade Hobbs lived with her parents Paul and Caroline and four siblings. The couple had been complaining about the traffic for some time, and had led a campaign to persuade Kent County Council to install a footbridge.

On 16 December, Jade was walking with her grandmother, Margaret Kuwertz, across the motorway. Her grandmother had looked across the road, and decided it was safe, but just before they managed to cross the other side, she was hit by an oncoming vehicle. Jade attempted to pull her grandmother to safety, but was also killed by the impact. Caroline Hobbs later recalled "Mum must've thought they could get across and hadn't seen the other car. And they were actually nearly across when the car hit them.

A footbridge has since been installed and named Jade's Crossing. It's in Detling, Kent and the footbridge crosses the A249, a major road which runs between Maidstone and Sheerness. Jade's mother, Caroline, subsequently campaigned for the crossing to be built, and won a Special Award at the 2003 Pride of Britain Awards for her efforts. *Source: National press

As an example of how messages work for me. The other night I did a group reading and an older lady came through to me who was speaking Italian. This bloke put his hand up and it turned out that they were cousins. The Nan was his mum's mum. I said to him, "Although she spoke very little English, you are actually fluent in Italian." He agreed. I asked, "Who's Maria?" and he wasn't sure, as I went on to say that it was something like a middle name and then all of a sudden, I said, "She's saying that she left you a property, or that there is a property in Sorrento." The man gasped as I went on to say that it was an old building, three storeys high and that it has fallen into disrepair. I told him that she wants you to go and sort it out. He confirmed, "yes, that's the plan. All of a sudden, I could see Pinocchio being carved. So, I said who is Giuseppe and he confirmed that was his name. I told him how I'd got his name. They [the Spirit world] don't necessarily tell me they show me pictures and I have to work it out. I knew that Giuseppe had carved Pinocchio in the story so that's how I got his name.

So, going back to the couple who had lost their daughter, they asked me if I would do a reading for a friend of theirs. Again, the cameras had been turned off and I got her son coming through. His name was Lee and he had been killed on a motorbike. The camera crew, although not filming, were still with us and intrigued. They said, "Oh I wish we'd got that reading on camera. The one you did first was good, but this one was incredible." I told them that's the difference when I'm not put under pressure. I told them I had to be cautious in the first reading as I knew it was going to go on TV and so I was understandably terrified of getting something wrong. It's like being a brilliant driver but failing your test because of nerves. I didn't want to go on TV and look stupid. Anyway, shortly afterwards I went to the toilet and in there was a tarot reader from one of the stalls at this psychic fair. He asked how I got on and did I get the daughter's nickname. So, I told him, yes I did and what it was.

A couple of weeks later I got a message from the couple which I'd originally read for the piece on the telly. The ones who had lost their daughter Jade. He asked if I told the tarot reader Jade's nickname, so I said yes I did. He said, "The bastard! After you'd gone, he kept on telling us he needed to give us a message. He said to me, "Would you understand the term Shady Lady? I just knew he hadn't got it from Jade." The poor man was disgusted. Unfortunately, that's how some people work.

As for the piece on the Telly, due to the editing it was terrible. It started with a piece from a Vicar saying you shouldn't talk to the dead, that it's evil. Then they panned around the hall with all of these weird looking people with flowing hair. Next you saw a tarot card reader placing cards on the table then they cut to the piece about me but left out the bit where I spoke of the Nan or the car coming up the motorway and it basically made me look bad.

The couple, Jade's parents, did their nut when it was aired as did the TV Production Company who originally put me forward for the filming. They phoned me and apologised personally for it. At the end of the day the couple I read for were over the moon and that's all that matters. I've never done anything since for the BBC. The couple eventually moved to France, and they still keep in touch with me.

[At this point, as Ronnie finished telling me about this couple, the hairs on the back of my neck stood up. I realised as the ghostwriter of Ronnie's book, that I had actually been to Jade's Crossing in Detling, 12 months earlier.

It was quite by chance before I'd even met Ronnie. I'd been staying nearby and passed the footbridge on several occasions during our stay. I remember I had looked up why it was called Jade's Crossing as I have a niece with the same first name. For some reason at the time, I had felt compelled to discover its history. Little did I know that a year later I'd be talking to a Medium, I'd never met before, about the same, sad piece of the past.]

I was reminded of a bizarre story in the gym the other day. I go there regularly and me and my mate Woody we were talking about another medium who has passed over now.

She lived at Burnham on Crouch and she was such a funny lady. Her name was Helania Briarly, she was a brilliant medium. If you caught her on a day when she was off-song, she could be useless. However, if she wanted to work, my God she was brilliant. I always got on really well with her. She always used to call me James Bond. I had hair then and was good looking – not the wreck I am nowadays!

Her house was a tip. When you went in she would always say, "Oh I'm decorating." I used to tell her, "You've been decorating for the last 20 fucking years! But she was funny, and she had the Mystic Meg haircut plus she used to have a funny stare. Years ago, she came to see me do a show. She always told me I could do this. She told me once she said, "You're special." This one time she went to this chap's dad's house to read for a few people. It turned out that his grandad was a stonemason and he done this work on an old church, carvings and stuff like that.

Anyway, he made a replica model of this church, and it stood in the room she was now in.

Unfortunately, this man had poured petrol over himself, chained himself up, and set light to himself. Helania went round there and as she stood in the room, she immediately said, "I'm on fire, I'm on fire!" she said, "And it's coming from that church!" Inside the model of the church was the newspaper cutting telling the story of this poor unfortunate chap committing suicide. The chap who had booked her apparently said, there is no way she could have known about his grandfather and his untimely death.

Helania was such a lovely woman. I remember she went out to Wales to help the police solve a murder case and she managed to help them to find where the victim was buried.

RONNIE BUCKINGHAM

CHAPTER 14

CAN A MEDIUM EVER RETIRE?

Can mediums ever retire? I don't think that a real, genuine medium can really, ever retire. If I take a week or a couple of weeks off from doing readings, they [the spirits] peck away at me. Then I find I'm giving messages to people willy nilly. It might be someone in a pub when we are in a bar having a quiet drink. Or even someone will pop round our house for something else and I get a message for them. I find that is the case especially on holiday.

Many a time we go away, and I find there's always a message which needs to be heard. Before I know it, I've sat next to someone, and I just know that they've lost a child. Or it could be I go somewhere and meet some others on the same trip, and I know that they have lost a husband or their dad. That's happened to me so many times. Saying that, I do know of other mediums who have retired. A chap called Bill Brockwell was a good, steady medium and he did retire several years ago and doesn't do it anymore.

I am semi-retired these days. I still do the odd readings and I still do some shows but just not as many as I used to. I can honestly say that I can't see the spirit world ever allowing me to retire fully. It's strange because I feel that they [the spirits] have given me enough money to have a decent life, but not enough money to be able to retire, in truth. So maybe that's how they keep you going. As long as there's a need out there and while I can still do what I do, I really can't see myself packing up anytime soon. This is an email I received from Eamon ...

Hi Ronnie,

I have just finished reading your first book and wanted to say thanks for helping me find some peace again. Since my partner and the love of my life passed away last year from cancer, I felt totally lost and so I immersed myself in the afterlife. I was desperately trying to find if it's true that we go on. I went to a couple of mediums for proof but came away more frustrated and with not much proof.

I was recommended to read your book and I'm so glad I did. You have left me in no doubt that we go on after here. Some of the stories and testimonies are mind blowing and I know one day I will be reunited with my beautiful partner.

Thank you so much for writing the book and bringing so much peace to so many people.

God bless you Ronnie, kind regards

Eamon

I hope by reading the testimonials in both this book and also my first book *Medium Rare*, you can see how life changing a reading can be for people. So, until the good Lord calls me home, whenever that may be, I'll continue to crack on doing what I'm doing. Just letting people know the truth that there really is life after death and that you can watch over your family and your loved ones once you pass on. Being able to prove that you will see them again, that's why I keep doing what I do.

Some mediums are really good and some unfortunately are not that great. If you think about it in life there are those who can get up and sing like Shirley Bassey and others who can't even hold a note at a karaoke party. I've seen some terrible readings done over the years. Obviously, I'm not going to name names but sometimes I think these so-called mediums are booked by venues just to fill up the seats and that's never a good idea. Better to do less dates but use really good, genuine mediums than have them more often with just random people who claim to have the gift.

Since I published my first book which sold 1000s of copies, I was even approached about perhaps turning my story into a film. I did book signings in Braintree and also in a pub which is local to me. I also took my books to my events. You can still buy it on Amazon. The feedback I got from people who read my first book *Medium Rare* was that it made me somehow more real to them.

Nicky and I have joked about taking copies with us when we go abroad on holidays and then my book will be an International book! We never have, just in case you're wondering. Knowing my luck, I'd still be at the resort and someone would read it, recognise me and then want me to give them a message while I'm supposed to be on my holidays!

When people meet me on holiday and say to me, what is it that you do. It's very hard, as what do you say? I just simply say, "Well I'm a medium." We've met several friends on holiday and of course everyone is fascinated by it. We went on a cruise, not so long ago, for my 70th birthday.

We were meant to be at sea for the New Year's Eve but we weren't. We were actually still in Southampton due to bad weather. It was too choppy for the ship to set out. So, if you've ever cruised, you'll know that everyone is herded onto the ship, up the gangway and you end up in a big meeting place called the Muster Point. Then you go up to your cabins. Nicky went off to sort our cabin out and I stayed where I was.

A lovely lady came along in a motorised wheelchair, and she had a carer with her. The lady's name was Kathleen and her carer was called Sue. We sat talking about cruises and I told her it was our first one. Kathleen said, "Oh you're going to love it!" She explained that she and her husband used to cruise together all the time. She told me that he had passed over and so I said, "Yes I know."

Kathleen looked a little taken aback and said, "What do you mean, you know?" I told her that I could sense him next to her. I told her then that I was a medium. Kathleen told me that she'd seen some very good mediums in the past. I told her that this man I could sense close by her was actually her third husband. I said he was the love of your life. She agreed with me and so I asked her, "Whose Tony?" Kathleen's face lit up, "That's him! That's my third husband." She said. I told her she only had the one daughter and that Tony her late husband had one son. I said, "That son, unfortunately has made your life a nightmare!" I told her that Tony was a member of a golf club and I described him perfectly and that she was now cruising in his memory. Kathleen's eyes welled up. She asked me, "Ronnie, does he mind?" I said what do you mean? She said, "Does my husband mind that I'm still going on cruises without him?"

I was able to reassure her that it was exactly what her late husband wanted her to do. I said to her, "He's telling me that he left you with quite a bit of money and that you can afford it. He wants you to enjoy it, but know that he still goes with you, in spirit." The carer Sue, said to me, "You've just made her holiday. She adored that man." I told her about the relationship they had had and the kind of things that they did together before he passed. I always tell it as it is with people. I can honestly say that if he'd told me he was upset with her cruising I would have told her.

My job is to pass messages on. I don't add to messages or subtract from them.

I just give them as they come. If I get a message when I'm not working like that, and it was put on me to deliver that message then that's what I'll do. They [the spirit world] knew that Kathleen needed to know that. 'Coz that was part of the jigsaw that was missing for her. His blessing for her lifestyle since he'd passed over and the fact that his love was still around her. It was a nice feeling for me to be able to do this for her. She was such a lovely, lovely woman. Despite being in an electric wheelchair, she never stopped smiling and kept herself looking so smart. A nice old soul.

Later into the cruise we would bump into them and as it was also my birthday whilst we were cruising Kathleen actually bought me a birthday card. Although I was away on a break I could just sense when Kathleen came towards me that day that she really needed to hear from her late husband. I can say that I didn't give messages to anyone else for the whole two weeks after that.

When I say that I can sense people let me explain that for you. I'm basically a clairsentient which means that when a spirit comes near me, I can feel what they were like. So, if someone was a spiteful, nasty person when they were living, I'll know it. If they were kind, quietly spoken or loud, boisterous or a depressed person I can feel all of that straight away. Next, I get a sense of them and by that, I mean that in my mind I can see them. Sometimes I can see them really clearly just like I can see a person in the flesh, but that's not very often.

I've had it where I can see that the person looks like someone and I can describe them by saying for example I said once, "Your dad I can see, and he looks just like Matt Monroe." So, I tend to know the person's size and hair colour. I've said before, "Your dad's got hair but it doesn't feel right to me. Did he wear a wig?" Then his relations will laugh and say, "Actually yes, he did."

A lady, Tracey, came up to me at a show I did recently, and she gave me a cuddle. She told me I'd changed her life and she couldn't thank me enough. She'd lost a child and I'd said that she'd go on to have another child. Her testimonial in her own words is featured [in Chapter 7] in this book. I told her it's ok, it's what I do. However, she insisted saying, "No it's more than that Ronnie, it goes deeper than that." She said, "I owe you so much!" I told her, "No you owe me nothing, nothing at all. I'm just glad that I can help."

I believe that you have to have a balance in your life, you can't let the mediumship take you over because it could so easily do that. You can't be the answers to people's prayers all the time, 24/7. I also make time to live my life too. We go out for meals with friends when we can. I still like all the things I used to like, I just can't do it as much anymore.

I've been doing this for a long time now. We are going back 28 years now. However, much time they'll [the spirits] still allot me, I'll still always do readings. There is a need for readings. It is a violent world out there. There is a lot of bad things going on. I think people need to know that there is a better world out there, somewhere else.

If you have the ability to reassure people of that, why would you not do it? It's like being a Doctor. You can retire but if you see someone in front of you having a heart attack you're not going to walk past and say, "Well I'm no longer a doctor" are you? You're going to steam in and do what you do. If I'm near someone who is hurting because they've lost a son or a daughter, husband, wife or whoever and they are suffering, and I know that I can take away that suffering that's what I'm going to do. That is what I was given the gift for. That's me. If I can help people, then I always will.

I look at what I've got, I have a nice house and drive a nice car and I wear Rolex watches. I've got a few quid in the bank. I'm not rich, but I'm not short of money and I realise I have a good life. I've got everything I need. I want to continue to help people who aren't so fortunate in life. I've always had a giving nature. I think it's because I was always dressed in secondhand clothes for years as a child and I had it hard. I was bullied at school because of the way I looked. I was one of those kids you didn't want to sit next to. I was always scruffy. I don't know if I was also smelly? I might have been that too! So, I understand what it's like and how that feels. My dad was a compulsive gambler, and we had no money. I was brought up in the East End of

London so I wasn't the only one I'm sure. That's why I became violent. Kids would take the piss out of me and the only way I could stop their taunts was by being violent.

If they knew they were going to get hit with something or even get bitten they'd think twice. In those early days I'd fight anything. I didn't care, I'd just steam in.

I do think that's why I went into thieving. I learnt a lot, but I weren't that good at it in truth. I also did an honest job in those days, working on building sites. If I wanted to buy myself a new shirt, I'd have to work for two weeks on the site. It was hard work too. They didn't have forklifts then either. You unloaded the bricks by hand, and it was back-breaking work for silly money. £15 a week then or something like that. I'd give my mum £5 or £6 of that each week for my board and lodgings.

I remember I also wanted to buy my own car. So, I became a thief and the money rolled in. You'd go out and you'd come away with a few £1000s. I was then able to afford a nice car and nice clothes. Of course, you come unstuck, and you go to prison and the wheels fall off for a while. It's all of the experiences which have led me to where I am now and to become the man I am today.

That final stint in prison finished me. Four years – FOUR YEARS! Remembering back to all those years ago. I was about to share a stinking cell with two other men lying on their bunks. By contrast earlier that day I'd been free to drive in my nice car in the sunshine, in my immaculate suit.

It was a gorgeous hot summer's day and I'd driven to Chelmsford courthouse in my sports car.

Now I faced being, once again, in a cramped cell with a pot for the three of us to piss in, in the corner and only allowed a shower once a week. I never went back to my life of crime after that.

CHAPTER 15

AUNTS AND UNCLES

Ronnie did a private reading for me in the past, way back in the early 2000's. However, this message from a public reading I attended with Ronnie is always with me, and I would just like to say thank you to him. He helped me so much that evening, especially with all of the emotions I was going through at that time. So here is what happened.

During the first half of the show, about 15 to 20 minutes into the evening, I had to put my coat on.

My aunt Joyce is the in the middle.

I felt so cold. My friend was seated next to me, and she felt the same. Ronnie stopped for a break, and then we all sat back down for the second half.

He gave some messages out and then stopped and pointed in my direction. Ronnie said he had to stop and come to where I was seated. He said that a lady had been patiently standing behind me. Ronnie said she had just shown him a harp.

Ronnie explained that it meant that someone had either just passed or is in the process of passing.

My father-in-law Keith who she was bringing the harp for.

That lady turned out to be my aunt Joyce. The harp was for my father-in-law Keith who I was caring for at that time as he had end stage lung cancer. He passed a week after that night. Ronnie also told me that my aunt was saying I would be ok and that things would get much better for me. I was so sad that night as two days previously my husband (now ex-husband) had walked out of our marital home, leaving me to care for his father! I also had to deal with the marriage break up. I can confirm that since that time my auntie Joyce was right, things have got much better for me.

So, thank you to Ronnie, my auntie Joyce was so right.

Many Thanks

Lesa Allen

Quite the Following …

I am blessed with a considerable following on my Facebook pages **Medium Ronnie Buckingham** and I get lots of positive feedback almost daily. Here's just an example of some of the posts people leave on my pages for which I am of course eternally grateful ….

Tina Butterfield

What can I say? Everyone said you were amazing and tonight I couldn't agree more. You were spot on with so many things it blew me away, thank you from the bottom of my heart ♥ my only regret, I wish I had recorded it maybe something to consider as trying to recall all the wonderful things you said xxx as Arnie says I'll be back x

Louise Lister

Ronnie is absolutely amazing. So accurate on so many levels there's no way he would know such detailed information. He is so gifted. X

Sandra Smith

Saw Ronnie last week for the first time and I have to say what a fantastic night and a fantastic message I got. He is by far the best medium I have seen in a long long while and I have been involved in spiritualism since 1986 when my husband passed over. He is fantastic. Looking forward to seeing you again Ronnie.

Fiona Hutchins

I had the pleasure of a private reading from Ronnie Buckingham this morning, I went in nervous but was put at ease right away. He was spot on with almost everything, and since I've been home and spoke to mum the names I wasn't sure of have now been told who they are, was amazing to hear my dad is happy and OK up there, and not just my dad who I was hoping to come through, but other family members also, so I was lucky, he had said things no one would never have known blew my mind, I left in shock but feeling relief and more happy knowing my dad is doing good. Thank you so much Ronnie xxxx

Mark Greensides is feeling peaceful.

Yesterday I was fortunate enough to have a private reading with medium Ronnie Buckingham. It was a very emotional and comforting experience and he has finally given me the peace I needed surrounding my dad's passing. Everything he said was spot on. He knew things that I've never told anyone else. Thank you Ronnie, you are a legend in the world of psychic reading and I very much look forward to seeing you in action again at one of your shows

Jacqueline Ann Scott-Burgin

Just home from an evening with Ronnie, an amazing man who linked me up with my sister and niece. He shared things that only they would know, I am still a little shell shocked. Thank you Ronnie you have an amazing talent and you are blessed. X

Kelly Lane

Thank you so much Ronnie you was amazing last night the first visit of many I think you told us things you couldn't have possibly known a massive thank you from myself Rico and Sheila

When my first book came out in 2016, I was delighted that so many not only read my book but took the time to also give it a 5-star review – I have over 500 of them now and it's still growing. So, I'd like to thank each and every one of you who took the time to put into words how you felt after reading *Medium Rare*. Here are just three of the most recent reviews from the Amazon site.

5.0 out of 5 stars Amazing

Reviewed in the United Kingdom on 2 March 2023

Verified Purchase

Ronnie you saved my soul, by chance I read you were coming to a place very near where I live, I just had this feeling that I absolutely had to be there. The information I read had some comments that said it was cancelled, I looked you up and emailed you directly, you got back to me and confirmed you would be there. I was the 2nd person you spoke to, my son came through who we had heartbreakingly lost a year before in car accident, you told me things that absolutely no-one could have known, the peace you have given me is immeasurable, I went on to have a private meeting with you, I honestly can't thank you enough, your gift is priceless, I dread to think what dark place I be in without you. I thank you with all my heart & soul I know my son is happy and he is ok. It's hard to put into words, thank you Ronnie thank you so very much Xxx

5.0 out of 5 stars "A truly amazing Book from start to finish of a very gifted Medium who is so Rare! The title of this book could not be more apt"

Reviewed in the United Kingdom on 22 December 2016

Verified Purchase

I have enjoyed getting to know Ronnie in his book Medium Rare. The book is a true insight to Ronnie's life and some of the hard knocks he had to face on his journey in life that has brought him to be the person he is today. Medium Rare is a truly inspiring book of Ronnie having to grow up in with not a lot of money in hard times who has grafted in life ducking & diving in life to earn a pound note. These knocks he has had to endure have truly molded the person he is today. The book portrays the lovely character of Ronnie who gives so much of his time in helping others with his gift of Mediumship so Rare!

Ronnie is a truly inspiring character to others and proves that you can go on to do some amazing things in life and turn life's negative situations into positive ones, Ronnie proves in his book that being a Spiritual Medium is a rare gift to have and the responsibilities that lie within what he gives to those is a very important part of his life and is a truly remarkable person and a very likeable Character. You honestly get to see another side of Ronnie that no one knew. I have enjoyed being on Ronnie's Journey in this book and yet to keep following such a beautiful person who is truly honest to himself and others. He is a very gifted Medium and the title of his book could not be more apt. What can I say but a truly enjoyable read from start to finish.

Brilliant Easy addictive read by very respected person, now! lol

Reviewed in the United Kingdom on 21 June 2017

Verified Purchase

Brilliant didn't put the book down. I first met Ronnie at "Dave's Gym", in Braintree in 1994 when he was doing the doors in Hackney. That gym is closed now. As I was asking for advice on Bicep curls as a young lad at 17 training for Army entrance, he was very kind with advice. He is a lovely guy and this comes across in the book. After I left the Army I worked in Epping where the Gov was Roy Shaw, so I related to, and knew the names, places etc in this book. I also used to see Ronnie at another gym in Braintree and used to chat to him. So where other books are stretched/padded out by ghost writers this book is definitely not. The book details how he got into spiritualist work for about 3/4 of it, ie his upbringing-criminal past, then the last quarter is about his experiences of guiding people, and their difficulties. It is a very versatile read, if you like Roy Shaw's "Pretty Boy", or "Frankie Fraser's" East End type crime book this is for you, but there is less violence in it, only one time outside the old King's nightclub is a violent scene mentioned, which is good for women who want to read these topics. The book chronicles his move from the East End to the rural fields of Essex, countless relationships lol, I lost track myself, to his very well known and respected work as a medium. His move to France is well documented, and the difficulties of living abroad comes across, as does his grit at learning-studying spiritualist work. The only let down is the book is not as well or professionally published ie not content, but paper, and bar codes, pictures don't look as good as rest in my extensive library. Many thanks R

AFTERWORD

The reason why I chose Stephanie Mackentyre to write this latest book of mine was because Ruthie Baker who wrote my first book *Medium Rare*, has been quite unwell for a long, long time. I talked about writing this next book, over two years ago. I was telling people that it would be written and published soon, but poor Ruth, though illness, could never write it. In the end I contacted Ruth and asked her if she'd mind if I got someone else to write this next book for me.

People were literally crying out for me to write another follow up book so of course she agreed. My first thought was to go online via Facebook and I asked my followers if anyone knew of someone who might be able to write for me. I was lucky in that instantly I got several names given to me. One person also suggested a website for ghostwriters which I also looked at. I spoke to a couple of prospective writers, both nice enough people. One man, in particular, was very nice. Then I got a message via Facebook from Steph [Mackentyre].

It turned out that although I'd never met or read for Steph, I did know her sister Mel and her sister's ex-husband Malcolm from when they were together. As a couple they came out to France when we lived there, and Malcolm fitted the kitchen for me. So that was an introduction in a way. So, I contacted Steph, and she came right back to me. Instantly we had a connection, and I loved the way she was, sharp as a tack. Not only had she written books before, so therefore knew about publishing, she just made me feel really at ease when I spoke to her.

I'd been toying with my first book *Medium Rare* which the title plays on steaks and mediumship. I was looking at calling the next one perhaps *Well Done* or perhaps *Ronnie Buckingham Open Door* or something like that.

Just speaking on the phone to Steph, this is how quick she is, straight away she came back with what is the title of this latest book – *Medium Rare to Well Done*. Now I think I'm quite quick, but I couldn't think of that, so that was it. Next, we had our first face-to-face meeting to discuss everything going forward and we got on like a house on fire. I even gave her a little reading at the end of that first meeting.

She's also been really keeping me up to date with the book progress from the word go. She understands that I'm an idiot when it comes to phones and Dictaphone recording and writing. So, she takes all that stress on her shoulders, so I don't have to worry, thankfully.

It just felt right. I immediately liked the woman, and we had a rapport. She really knows her stuff. She's a very busy, but intelligent and kind person and so there she is, she has written this second book of mine.

Steph Mackentyre says ....

When I first met Ronnie, it was at his home in Braintree. Nicky, his lovely wife answered the door and they both made me feel so welcome from the very beginning. I was interested to find out just how the messages come through to Ronnie so he gave me a demonstration. Both in the form of a reading and in front of me he also he contacted his own spirit guide. Ronnie told me,

"I receive my messages via my spirit guide who I am in communication with a lot. It's a man, and I chat to him, and he'll also tell me off if I need it! I communicate with him via a pendulum."

[At this point Ronnie takes off the crucifix he wears around his neck.] "Watch this, if it rotates clockwise it means yes. If he wants to tell me no, then he rotates my pendulum anticlockwise. If he doesn't want me to answer something, then it will swing backwards and forwards."

[I watch his hand to make sure it's not moving] Ronnie says a quick prayer to his guide asking for protection and proceeds to ask his spirit guide the following;

"Are you present, dear Guide?" [The crucifix swings clockwise immediately.]

"Am I sitting in this room with another man?" [The crucifix changes direction and swings anticlockwise.]

"With another lady?" [Back the crucifix on the gold chain rotates clockwise.]

"Is she family to me?" [Once again it changes direction as Ronnie's hand above remains completely still.]

"Is she here to write a book?" [It begins to rotate clockwise once more.]

"Will it be a good selling book?" [It continues to spin around in a clockwise direction, just a little faster.] Ronnie explains, "The faster it goes that's a bigger yes."

"You're happy with what we've put into this book so far?" [The chain with the gold cross at the bottom is still swinging around clockwise.]

Ronnie finishes by saying to his Spirit Guide, "Thank you dear friend and God bless. A clockwise swing would be a good enough goodbye for me." [The chain swings around clockwise once again for the final time.]

He goes on to explain …

"So, I talk to him like that. If I'm troubled about something. For example, I do tend to swear quite a bit when I'm doing my shows. Let's just say my humour it's a bit tight. Often, I think back over the evening, and I worry thinking, Fuck me! Did I really say that on stage earlier tonight? When I get home, I'll speak to my Spirit Guide and say things like, did I swear too much tonight? The answer always comes back no. He loves it. I ask him should I carry on giving readings out the way I do, and he says, Yup. You can see why I have earned the nickname of the *Comedian Medium*."

I've also seen my spirit guide; his name is White Eagle. I have seen him standing at the end of my bed on occasions. He was a red Indian. Believe me I've always taken the piss out of people who say they have a Red Indian guide. However, I saw him, standing there in buck skins with only two feathers in a headband on the back of his head. Just a tiny little man, maybe only 5ft 2ins? His face looked like granite. It looked a thousand years old. Very strong jawline. He gave me the most beautiful smile.

When I saw him in our bedroom, I was wide awake, and he was literally standing there at the foot of my bed. He just smiled at me. I just smiled back and then he nodded at me and off he went. I knew instantly who he was as well. White Eagle was very famous in his day. You have White Eagle Lodge which is a famous spiritual lodge dedicated to him. He does great by me.

He'll tell me off sometimes. I might say after reading, I wasn't too pleased with the way things went tonight and he'll agree with me saying no me neither! I might ask was it because the crowd was difficult and he'll say, No! I'll ask was it me being off form or not so good and he'll say, yes. Other times when I know I've been bang on form it spins round really fast clockwise, meaning well done.

I swear sometimes just to break the tension in the room at the beginning of a night. I can go on stage and say to the audience, "Good Evening!" And there's just a quiet ripple around the room. I'll come back with, "For Fuck Sake I'm gonna be speaking to spirit people who sound more alive than you do tonight!" Then they all laugh, and it puts people at their ease.

Steph Mackentyre says …Ronnie said that he'd like to give me a reading at the end of our first meeting. I told him I would be happy to write the book without a reading as it was my job to make sure that his own words shone out of the pages of this book.

However, he insisted saying, 'It's very important to me that you believe I am able to do what other people are saying I can do." With that he took my right hand in his to make a connection. As he let go of it, he told me that he sensed my father was drawing close by. Before

I had a chance to confirm that he was indeed in spirit, he blind-sided me by describing my Mother, who had only recently passed over. He could have said something like oh she's a sweet little old lady and sends her love etc. Instead, he told me that he didn't particularly like her energy! That she was the sort of person to say hurtful things to you to have an effect on you.

I was so shocked, as it was completely true, and my Mother had only passed away literally a few months earlier. I was feeling very guilty and rather sad that I'd not yet shed a single tear. He went on to say that because of this I'd had a difficult time as a child, also true. As I sat there literally rooted to the sofa, he named my mum's two brothers who are still living. Not just the first letter of their names but their actual names, one of which is Ronald. Ronnie said, "They [the spirit world] are pointing to me! Is he called Ron? No hang on it's Ronald." He also told me that I was married to Stephen and the fact it's spelt with a PH which is also completely true. Steve as he likes to be called and I have been married for 10 years this year.

Then he almost tipped me over the edge, I managed to hold back only because I was there in a professional capacity. He told me he could see a small dog, more of a spaniel sized dog. To start with he couldn't tell the breed and then he said, "They are showing me black and white together, is it a Collie dog?" We'd lost our beloved Bonnie dog, who was indeed a border collie, just smaller than most, under a year ago.

Steph Mackentyre

# RONNIE BUCKINGHAM

A few more pictures from the Buckingham family album!

Nicky and I on a cruise to celebrate my 70th

Me on a boys holiday in Portugal next to me is Josh, Steve, Jim Bob, Craig and my brother Lee

My brother Micheal with his cab on the left is Pat, Jim Bob, Audrey and next to my brother is Vic

My daughter Marie and I at her wedding

Me with my daughter Vicki at Marconato Restaurant for her birthday

Me with Vicki as a child

My brother Michael, his son Lee and my daughter Vicki

Vicky and her husband Dave

Marie with her husband Trevor

My daughter Sarah with my daughter Marie

Vicki with her eldest son, Ronnie

Nicky, Me and her daughter (like a daughter to me) Amy

Nicky's family at one of their parties!

My grandson George (Vicki's son) above

My grandson Ronnie with his mum's (Vicki) wolf dog

Me with (Vicki's Son) my grandson Billy

My granddaughter Jessica (Vicki's daughter)

My granddaughters: (Sarah's older girls) Aurelia and Seraphine

Sarah's youngest daughter Allegra

My grandson Brandon with his daughter Bella Mae. She's my great granddaughter and my daughter Marie's granddaughter

My beloved dog Bandit (above)

Bandit and Bella together

Albere the One-Eyed French Cat

Me and Nicky horsing around

Raising £5k for the British Heart Foundation

Me in action with help from the spirit world

Every night brings different messages, all bringing proof of the afterlife

(Above) My friend of 60 years Paul Stanley and below Paul and I aged 10

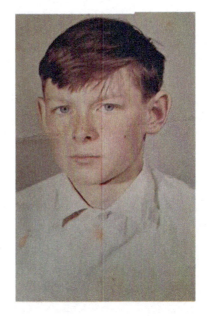

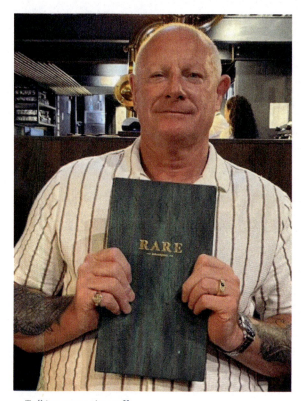

Talking some time off

The Opening Day of Cawston College in Norfolk

Me outside the College with the owner Steve Barry

Steve Barry and I about to address the crowd inside the College

This photograph was sent to me by a lady back in the day whose son died in a motorbike accident. She took this picture of his grave and when it was reproduced you can see there is the spirit of a motorbike with someone riding it just to the left

RONNIE BUCKINGHAM

Just as I was finalising this book, we lost a dear friend of ours very suddenly. I'd like to dedicate this page to him. Much loved by us and his wife Sharon and all of his family. Such a lovely man. RIP mate X

Kevin Pestell

5th April 1961 – 20th May 2024

With this book I've tried to emphasise that there really is life after death. It's not about fortune telling. I hope that this book not only touches those that have been to see me but also touches those people who will never see me but have just read this book. I'd like them to know that their loved ones do live on and that they can look over them. I'd like to say to you as the reader of this book, be kind to all those that you meet and try to enjoy your life. I've learnt a lot in life and that for me is the most important lesson I can pass onto you.

Always treat people the way you want to be treated yourself. Try to smile through everything, because everything is a test. Life is a difficult thing and every life you live is all about learning lessons. As you will have read, I've had a lot of illnesses and a lot of conditions to deal with myself. I try to see them as a positive thing rather than a negative thing and I fight to get through them, which is something I think we all need to do. I also hope that this book helps to take away some of the fear. Not of dying, because there isn't death, but there is a fear of going into the next life.

I'm 70 years old now so I'm slowing down but I'm just so thankful for the wonderful people who have had faith in me. I'd like to thank everyone for their wonderful feedback and for the way that I have been accepted by so many people and taken to their hearts for the work I've done for them. It really does mean an awful lot to me.

God bless you all, stay safe and stay well and always remember that the loved ones you have lost are never far away.

Love Ronnie xx

For all the latest information about forthcoming events and some more of Ronnie's fascinating history check out his new website www.ronniebuckingham.co.uk

You can also follow him by joining the Facebook group

Medium Ronnie Buckingham

ABOUT THE AUTHORS

Ronnie Buckingham is the author of *Medium Rare* and also now this book *Medium Rare to Well Done*. After many years living a life of crime he has finally found his life's purpose as a healer of hearts and an advocate for life after death. Ronnie has worked with spirit for the past 20+ Years and this work has taken him all over Europe. He has also appeared on both television and radio on many occasions and been featured in many magazine articles. He has given mediumship demonstrations to large groups and to individuals and many of those people who have gained comfort from his messages have since become lifelong friends.

He's not your run-of-the-mill medium, often surprising his audience with his cockney humour, his say-it-like-it-is style of giving messages and his abundant tattoos. Ronnie has turned many a sceptic, who has come along for the 'entertainment', into a true believer in the afterlife.

Although now in his 70th year Ronnie has cut back on many of his readings and shows, you can still contact him via his website **www.ronniebuckingham.co.uk or follow him via his Facebook group Medium Ronnie Buckingham which has to date over 17,000 followers*** *At the time of printing this book

Stephanie Mackentyre is a Writer, Publisher, Author & Podcaster.

Her latest book due to be released in 2024 is **Beyond the Bucket** *- A how-to guide for charities to get noticed and increase funding. It is an essential guide for charities and non-profit organisations who need to work through the minefield of available free media both online and via traditional outlets.*

With over 35 years of experience, interviewing people as a radio presenter and also a features writer, writing about other people's life experiences, Stephanie has plenty of stories to tell.

She has a passion for the theatre and each week she also hosts the Ruby Shoes Podcast, featuring the latest entertainment news and interviews across East Anglia. Follow @StephMackentyre for news on future forthcoming podcasts and book releases.

Printed in Great Britain
by Amazon